Animals are Souls too!

❧ ALSO BY HAROLD KLEMP ❧

The Art of Spiritual Dreaming

Ask the Master, Books 1 and 2

Autobiography of a Modern Prophet

The Book of ECK Wisdom

The Call of Soul

Child in the Wilderness

Contemplation Seeds on the Temple of ECK

A Cosmic Sea of Words: The ECKANKAR Lexicon

ECK Essentials

ECK Masters and You: An Illustrated Guide

ECK Wisdom Temples, Spiritual Cities, & Guides: A Brief History

Is Life a Random Walk?

The Living Word, Books 1, 2, 3, and 4

A Modern Prophet Answers Your Key Questions about Life, Books 1, 2, and 3

Past Lives, Dreams, and Soul Travel

Soul Travelers of the Far Country

The Sound of Soul

Spiritual Exercises for the Shariyat, Book One

Spiritual Exercises for the Shariyat, Book Two

The Spiritual Exercises of ECK

The Spiritual Laws of Life

The Temple of ECK

Those Wonderful ECK Masters

Welcome to the Wonderful World of ECK! Your Membership Guidebook

The Wind of Change

Wisdom of the Heart, Books 1, 2, 3, and 4

Your Road Map to the ECK Teachings: ECKANKAR Study Guide, Volumes 1 and 2

Youth Ask a Modern Prophet about Life, Love, and God

The MAHANTA Transcripts Series

Journey of Soul, Book 1

How to Find God, Book 2

The Secret Teachings, Book 3

The Golden Heart, Book 4

Cloak of Consciousness, Book 5

Unlocking Your Sacred Puzzle Box, Book 6

The Eternal Dreamer, Book 7

The Dream Master, Book 8

We Come as Eagles, Book 9

The Drumbeat of Time, Book 10

What Is Spiritual Freedom?, Book 11

How the Inner Master Works, Book 12

The Slow Burning Love of God, Book 13

The Secret of Love, Book 14

Our Spiritual Wake-Up Calls, Book 15

How to Survive Spiritually in Our Times, Book 16

The Road to Spiritual Freedom, Book 17

Spiritual Lessons from Living, Book 18

The Immortality of Soul Series

The Awakened Heart

The Awakening Soul

HU, the Most Beautiful Prayer

The Language of Soul

Love—The Keystone of Life

The Loving Heart

The Spiritual Life

Touching the Face of God

Truth Has No Secrets

Stories to Help You See God in Your Life

The Book of ECK Parables, Volumes 1, 2, and 3

Stories to Help You See God in Your Life, ECK Parables, Book 4

☙ Books by Paul Twitchell ❧

ECKANKAR—The Key to Secret Worlds

The ECK-Vidya, Ancient Science of Prophecy

The Flute of God

Herbs: The Magic Healers

The Key to ECKANKAR

The Spiritual Notebook

Stranger by the River

The Tiger's Fang

☙ A Selection of ECKANKAR Reference Books ❧

A Cosmic Sea of Words: The ECKANKAR Lexicon

ECK Essentials

ECK Masters and You: An Illustrated Guide

ECK Wisdom Temples, Spiritual Cities, & Guides: A Brief History

The Shariyat-Ki-Sugmad, Book One

The Shariyat-Ki-Sugmad, Book Two

Spiritual Exercises for the Shariyat, Book One

Spiritual Exercises for the Shariyat, Book Two

The Spiritual Exercises of ECK

The Spiritual Laws of Life

Those Wonderful ECK Masters

Welcome to the Wonderful World of ECK! Your Membership Guidebook

The Wonder within You (for youth)

☙ New to ECK? ❧
by Harold Klemp

ECK Wisdom Series

ECK Wisdom on Conquering Fear

ECK Wisdom on Dreams

ECK Wisdom on Health and Healing

ECK Wisdom on Inner Guidance

ECK Wisdom on Karma and Reincarnation

ECK Wisdom on Life after Death

ECK Wisdom on Prayer, Meditation, and Contemplation

ECK Wisdom on Relationships

ECK Wisdom on Solving Problems

ECK Wisdom on Soul Travel

ECK Wisdom on Spiritual Freedom

ECKANKAR's Spiritual Experiences Guidebook

Animals are Souls too!

HAROLD KLEMP

ECKANKAR
Minneapolis
Eckankar.org

Animals Are Souls Too!

Printed in USA

Photos by Allen Anderson, pp. 47, 167; Tammy Attama, front-cover background, p. 223; Kim Calvert, back cover; Art Galbraith, p. 255; Justine Watkins, p. 1; Bree Renz, p. 123; John Villemonte, p. 111; and Kristy Walker, pp. 75, 95, 183, 205. Animals Are Souls logo designed by Connie Kroskin.

Second edition—2023

This book has been authored by and published under the supervision of the MAHANTA, the Living ECK Master, Sri Harold Klemp. It is the Word of ECK.

MAHANTA

Library of Congress Cataloging-in-Publication Data

Names: Klemp, Harold, author.
Title: Animals are souls too! / Harold Klemp.
Description: Second edition. | Chanhassen, MN : Eckankar, [2023] | Summary: "Author Harold Klemp, spiritual leader of Eckankar, shares true-life stories from around the world-stories which show animals displaying an astonishing depth of awareness and serving as carriers of divine love. Animals share a divine kinship with us. We're each Soul, a divine spark of God"-- Provided by publisher.
Identifiers: LCCN 2022062148 | ISBN 9781570435317 (paperback)
Subjects: LCSH: Eckankar (Organization)--Doctrines. | Animals--Religious aspects--Eckankar (Organization)
Classification: LCC BP605.E3 K52 2023 | DDC 299/.93--dc23/eng/20230119
LC record available at https://lccn.loc.gov/2022062148

♾ This paper meets the requirements of ANSI/NISO Z39.48-1992 (Permanence of Paper).

Contents

Introduction

*I*f you have a pet, you are aware of the bond of love between yourself and your pet. This bond of love exists because you are Soul—a particle of God sent here to gain spiritual experience. Ultimately, to learn how to give and to receive divine love.

What most people don't realize is their pet is also Soul. Animals are Souls too.

Soul exists because God loves It. It's very simple. And when two Souls set up a bond of love, it is stronger and more enduring than eternity. It doesn't matter if the two Souls are human beings or if one of them happens to be a bird, a dog, a cat, or another animal form.

I have observed, and maybe you have too, that some pets seem to have a higher state of consciousness than many people. When an animal does something that looks very human—showing compassion or love and mercy to its owner who is sick or feeling sorrow—some say it's just instinct. But actually, that animal is far above some people because it can show and express God's love.

As the stories in this book reveal, animals can love unconditionally. This is divine love in action, a love that's there no matter what you say or how bad you feel that day.

You, me, our pets—we are all Soul dwelling here in the world of nature. As you read the pages to come, you will see that nature itself reflects the laws of ECK, the Holy Spirit. We can observe the working of Divine Spirit in the habits of birds, the cycles of plants, and the instincts of reptiles and mammals.

All sing the glory of God; all teach the secrets of life.

CHAPTER ONE

Animals and Divine Love

The Butterfly

A family was moving from the East Coast to the West Coast of the United States. As soon as they had settled into their new home, the mother knew that this had been the wrong move to make.

Her husband's new company was very unfriendly toward him, and everything about their new home felt wrong. Over the weeks, the woman became more and more unhappy.

One evening just before dinner, her daughter came into the kitchen. In her hand on a little piece of paper, there sat a butterfly. It was a wood nymph, a brown butterfly with dark spots on its wings.

"Mommy, look what I found outside," the daughter said.

"Mommy, look what I found outside," the daughter said.

The mother looked at the butterfly. She could tell it was just about at the end of its life. "Before dark, you ought to put the butterfly back outside," she said. So the little girl carefully carried the butterfly outside and placed it where the family could see it from the kitchen window.

Later when her daughter had gone to bed, the mother looked outside. *Maybe I ought to bring the butterfly inside*, she thought. *It's not going to live very long, but it shouldn't have to be out there in the cold. It could be here in the kitchen by the stove where it's warm.* So she went out and brought it inside the house.

3

The next morning when she came down to the kitchen, the woman saw that little butterfly was still alive. "Brave little thing," the woman said. "It just seems to sit there. But it will probably die pretty soon."

When afternoon came, the butterfly was still looking at her from its perch in the kitchen. "Maybe there's something I can do for it," the woman said. "Maybe it's hungry. What do you feed a butterfly?" She didn't know. She thought she'd try putting a little honey on her finger. She diluted a drop of honey with water and held it near the butterfly's mouth. A tiny tongue came out, and the butterfly ate the honey.

What do you feed a butterfly? She didn't know.

The next day when the woman tried to feed the butterfly, it had more strength. It came toward her.

Pretty soon the butterfly didn't want to get off the woman's hand when feeding time was over. It would stay for a while because this tiny creature began to love her. And the woman began to love it back.

One day, she was wearing a woolen garment, and the butterfly got one of its legs caught in the wool. The leg got pulled off. Now it had only five legs. The woman was horrified. "Oh no, what have I done?"

But even with five legs, the little butterfly would always come out to meet her as much as it could.

The butterfly was nearing the end of its three-week visit. One night it looked like it was ready to go. Its wings were quivering, so the woman stayed with the butterfly for a long time. Then finally she said good-bye to it and went to bed feeling sad.

Next morning when she got up, the butterfly was still alive, but barely. So she sang *HU*, an uplifting, ancient love song to God. She put the butterfly on her finger and sang very gently to it with love. Soon after, the butterfly passed on.

The woman marveled about the way this little being had transformed her entire family in just three weeks. Her unhappiness was gone. The butterfly had brought joy into the home, and this joy was infectious. It caught her husband and her daughter, and especially it caught the woman herself.

Not only that, but the butterfly had taught her some important lessons. Such as patience. And endurance without complaining. It had showed her a strong desire to live. But most of all, it showed her how to love. During the three weeks of its visit, the butterfly transformed her from a person who was depressed and unhappy. It began to open her heart and awaken the love within the woman again.

Sometimes the Holy Spirit sends other Souls to minister to people.

Whether or not your philosophy or religion accepts Souls in forms other than the human is unimportant. If you can accept reincarnation and the fact that Soul takes on many different bodies—and some of these Souls are better vehicles for love than some people—you will find much joy and happiness in your own life. You'll also find a greater understanding of God's creation.

The Bear and the Berries

*M*any years ago, a man worked at a paper mill in a remote town near the US-Canadian border. To do their shopping in the nearest city, the towns-people had to drive quite a distance along a deserted highway.

One weekend, the man started the trip to the city to pick up supplies. On a stretch of road that ran through the forest, he saw parked cars and a group of people gathered around a path that led to the woods. There wasn't much excitement in that remote area, so naturally the man was curious to see what had drawn so many people. He parked his car and walked over to join them.

As he worked his way through the crowd, he saw a big black bear sitting on its haunches, its front paws up in the air. Right away he spotted the problem.

The bear had thorns stuck in its paws.

Being a practical sort of person, the man hurried back to his car and got a pair of pliers. He then re-turned to the bear and pulled out the thorns. As soon as the man finished, the bear got back down on all fours and sprinted off into the woods. Gradually the people got back in their cars and went about their business.

The man continued on to the city and did his shopping. Three hours later he started back home along the same route. When he reached the spot

He saw a big black bear sitting on its haunches, its front paws up in the air. Right away he spotted the problem.

7

where he had seen the bear earlier, he again noticed a bunch of cars parked at the side of the road.

I wonder what's going on now, he thought.

He parked his car, worked his way through the crowd, and found the very same black bear, this time intently examining the face of each person before him.

Suddenly the bear saw the man who had pulled the thorns from his paws. The curious crowd watched as the bear turned and ran a short distance into the woods, went behind a bush for a moment, and came running back with two pails of blueberries dangling from his mouth.

He went right over to the man and stood patiently in front of him, the handles of the pails clasped between his teeth, until finally the man got the hint and took the blueberries from him. His deed accomplished, the bear quickly turned around and headed back into the woods.

Truth is often stranger than fiction, and these things do happen. But where would a bear get two pails of blueberries?

A bear in the woods can get anything he wants. I suspect there's another story behind this one that may someday be revealed. It has to do with a berry picker out in the woods alone who suddenly sees a huge black bear standing nearby on its hind legs. With a ferocious roar, the bear probably says something like, "Sir, may I have those blueberries, please?" And being an openhearted person, the berry picker no doubt replies, "Certainly; I can pick some more later"—and runs off screaming.

The man who helped the bear didn't have any fear because he was filled with love. When one of the creatures of ECK, the Holy Spirit, was in need of help, he gave it without hesitation.

And once given, the gift of love had to be returned.

The only kind of love worth anything at all is pure love. When we can see this pure love as divine love, we come to know that there is enough for everyone, for all creatures and all things.

The man who helped the bear didn't have any fear because he was filled with love.

9

Bird Hug

A woman had been working for many years, when she came to a point in her life when she had to go through a number of surgeries. Because of the surgeries, she had to quit her job. And when she quit work, her source of income dried up. She'd been a postal worker, so she got a pension from the post office. But she and her husband were not able to live at the same level they had before.

To make it worse, with less money, her husband began to scold her constantly. She was sick. She had just come through several operations. She couldn't take care of him as she had before—serve him hand and foot—and he was complaining all the time. "Why don't you do this for me anymore?" he'd ask.

Along with all this misery, the woman was no longer able to take care of her grandson. She loved the little fellow, but she was too weak from the surgeries to care for him.

The woman grew more and more unhappy. It got so bad that when someone would come up to her, she'd begin to cry, right out of the blue. And she didn't know what to do about it.

One day, she went to visit her neighbor. The young woman was a licensed day-care person. She was taking care of tiny two-year-olds. The woman walked up to the gate, and her neighbor let her in. All the children came up to her and said hello.

The woman began to cry, because she realized how much she missed her grandson.

In the front yard was an open cage with a beautiful, large, white cockatiel. The woman was standing close to the cage when a very unusual thing happened. The cockatiel leaned over and kissed her on the cheek.

"I've never seen him do that to anyone before," the neighbor said, very surprised.

Next, the bird put out its wing and wrapped it around the woman's shoulder.

The neighbor said, "Look at that. This bird has never kissed anybody on the cheek before, and it has certainly never put its wing around anybody's shoulder."

They marveled about what had happened, and the woman went back home, her spirits lightened.

We tend to think of humans as the pinnacle of evolution. This may be true of biological evolution, but it is not necessarily the case from a spiritual perspective. Many Souls in the animal form are already highly evolved spiritually. They can give and receive divine love in a way that many humans would not understand.

In this case, Soul in a cockatiel's body was answering a call from the Holy Spirit, which was saying, "Here's a fellow Soul that needs your love and comfort."

The bird was a clear instrument for the Holy Spirit to convey divine love to this woman who had had her share of hardships. This is how the Holy Spirit passes comfort to Its creation. It gives love.

And the woman was comforted. She realized she was not alone. That the bird putting its wing around her shoulder was assurance from the ECK, the Holy Spirit, that divine love and protection were always with her.

The bird was a clear instrument to convey divine love to this woman.

The Scottish Farmer

A farmer in Scotland had a large herd of cows. He and his wife treated these cows like their children. Every morning they'd come out to feed and milk them. They would call each cow by name and give them little treats. They'd pet them. The cows loved the farmer and his wife, and the couple loved the cows.

One day the farmer got on his tractor and drove out into the field to check on a newborn calf. This was risky because a neighbor's bull had been brought over for breeding purposes and was loose in the field.

When the bull saw the farmer, he charged the tractor and knocked the farmer off and began to gore him. The farmer went unconscious.

When he woke up some time later, he found that his herd of cows had made a tight circle of protection around him. The bull was furious, and he charged the cows again and again, trying to break through that circle. Some of the cows were badly hurt, and a few died from internal bleeding.

When he woke up, he found his herd of cows had made a tight circle of protection around him.

But the circle of cows stayed until someone arrived to help the farmer.

As the man told the story later, he began to cry. "People who say that cows are stupid don't know what they're talking about," he said.

This man knew that God's love is larger than just a love for humans. It stretches from one human to

15

another, of course, but it also stretches from humans to animals, to birds, to fish, and even to a herd of cows.

In case you haven't discovered it, the whole purpose in living—the whole purpose of God's plan—is so each of us learns how to love.

And where does love begin?

It begins with those who are near and dear to us. If we can't love them, how are we ever going to love God? And before we can love those who are near and dear to us, both people and animals, we've got to learn to love ourselves.

The Peaceful Bees

A woman liked to set food out on her porch for dogs, cats, and birds. Every morning the birds perched on her windowsill and chirped their signal that it was time for breakfast. As soon as she stepped outside with the food, all the birds and cats and dogs gathered around.

But lately the woman had noticed that a group of bees liked to come around and eat the cat food too.

The woman noticed a group of bees liked to come and eat the cat food too.

Thinking about this scene, I became curious. "If the cats and bees eat the same food," I said, "do they eat together out of the same dish, or do they take turns? Who gets to eat first?"

The woman explained that the cats ate the food while the bees flew around them in circles, waiting for an opening.

Not long after, the woman heard some chilling news reports on TV. Swarms of killer bees were moving north from South America and Mexico. These killer bees were reported to attack anything in their path, and they especially like to eat meat.

Realizing how much the bees that hung around her porch liked to eat cat food, the woman got nervous. What if these were killer bees?

She decided she would continue her small service to life. So she kept setting out the food every morning, and the creatures gathered around to enjoy it.

What if these were killer bees?

The days went by, and neither she nor any of the cats ever got stung.

The woman had protection because of the love that came through her. The other creatures sensed this love.

Scientists say that the laws of physics make the world go round. This may be so at one level. But at a higher level, in an absolute sense, it is love that makes the world go round.

Love and love alone.

Bag Lady

One day a man in Texas realized that he really didn't know much about divine love. So in his contemplation he asked the MAHANTA, the inner side of myself, "Show me divine love."

Not long afterward, he was helping a friend clean up his yard. There were some empty soda cans behind the house, and a woman was collecting them. To the man, she looked one cut above a bag lady. This bag lady was willing to work for her food. She was collecting cans, and she had a little dog with her.

The man saw the little dog and called it over, and the dog came very carefully. It sniffed at his hand and stood to get petted. Then the woman came over, and they talked a little bit about one thing or another.

As he was about to leave, the man looked into the woman's eyes. They were so clear and sincere. As a matter of fact, so were the dog's eyes.

He realized that this woman had a special love for her dog, and the dog had a special love for her. Probably no one in society loved her except the dog.

"Thank you for being so kind to my dog," the woman said.

During the next few days as the man did the spiritual exercises he'd learned in the teachings of Eckankar, he tried to focus his attention on different things. But the face of this woman and her little dog

In contemplation he asked, "Show me divine love."

always came back to him. The woman's face was always in his inner vision.

The man had been trying to find the meaning of love. He'd found it in himself to approach the woman through her dog, to be kind to the dog. And this in turn allowed him to give and receive love from the old lady.

It only took a few days for the man to realize that this was divine love. This was the love he'd asked to be shown.

Divine love is a very humble love; it's a true love. Don't look too high, because you won't find it. The love of God is often very low where no one will look for it. And this is why so few people find it.

A Chunk of Bread

A woman wrote to me. Her life had pretty much caught up with her and stomped her down. She was fed up. In her letter she said, "Harold, tell it to me straight. What do I need to know?"

I wrote back to her, "Do one thing each day for love alone. Don't expect any kind of reward."

When the woman got my letter, she was so excited. She called her friend to go to the mall with her so she could tell her all about the letter over tea or a snack.

But her friend said, "I can't go to the mall with you; I've got a meeting." So the woman went alone.

She was sitting by an outdoor fountain in a courtyard, enjoying her tea. The letter had opened up the love inside her, but there was nobody to share it with. She wanted to spill this love across the table. But the ECK, the Holy Spirit, wanted to teach her how to give love in the most humble way.

Suddenly, the woman noticed a small flock of birds hovering around the fountain. Remembering the message in the letter, she said, "How nice it would be if I had some bread to feed the birds."

And just like that, out of the sky came a chunk of bread!

It hit her on the shoulder and fell to the ground in front of her. "Heaven does provide," she laughed, and she fed the birds.

She said, "How nice it would be if I had some bread to feed the birds."

After she'd fed them all the bread, her friend walked up. "The meeting was cancelled," she said. "We can have lunch after all."

The woman's lesson was to do one little thing each day for love and love alone, without any expectation of reward. What a difference it can make. If you do this, you'll find life gives you more and more.

A Simple Exercise to Spiritualize Yourself

*I*f times are hard for you during the day, you can spiritualize yourself by singing *HU* (pronounced like the word *hue*), an ancient name for God.

Sing it on a long, drawn-out note. But sing it with love for God. It's a simple prayer song that will lift you and help you through.

Singing this ancient love song to God will help you become a better person, in all ways and in all places, for all beings.

When you sing *HU*, you agree to let Divine Spirit do what is best for you.

CHAPTER TWO

Relationships between Humans and Animals

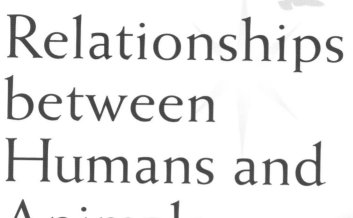

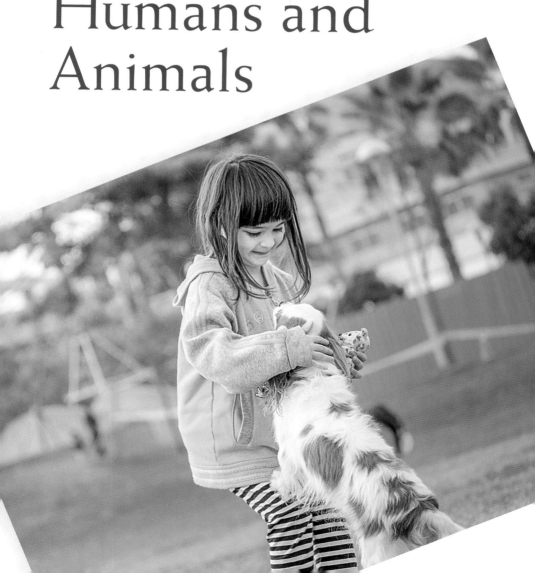

Cats and Dogs

*C*ats need a lot of freedom. They know it, and they demand it. Being self-centered and having a lot of opinions, cats enjoy things a certain way. They like to run the household.

And if you don't give cats their freedom, they are very unhappy creatures.

Say you are returning from a vacation. Your cat will immediately let you know if you've mistreated him by not giving him the proper kennel or place to stay while you were gone. He may let you pet him; he may not.

The cat says, "So. Where've you been? Had a good time?"

Then maybe he won't come out of his cage. He says, "Look at this crummy place you've kept me. I hope you had a good time, but you never think of anybody else. I think I'm going to stay in here and die."

You have to reach in, grab the cat, and pull him out to take him home. The cat allows this without too much scratching because he really does want to go home.

With a dog it's different: When you get back from vacation, your dog comes running up to you, tongue hanging out.

"So glad to see you, so glad to see you," the dog says. "Glad you're back. Let's go home."

Being self-centered and having a lot of opinions, cats enjoy things a certain way.

I don't think a dog has opinions. A dog has love. Dogs are generations and lifetimes ahead of cats as far as divine love goes.

Spiritually if you want to have a role model and don't want to look to other people or a Master, look to dogs. Dogs have a good relationship with life, generally.

Dogs are coworkers. They say, "What can I do for you? Bring your slippers? You don't want the paper? I'll get it anyway."

Dogs are more like what we work toward in Eckankar.

One day people will become Coworkers with God after they have had all the experience. Dogs are there already.

My account of the differences between cats and dogs is a bit tongue-in-cheek. But the point I am making is very simple: Animals are Souls too. Every variety of pet—cat, dog, or whatever—is an embodiment of Soul, just like you and me.

Each is individual, and each can act as a channel or an instrument for divine love.

Charlie and Moon

*C*harlie is a dog, and Moon is a cat. Charlie's waking hours are devoted to one goal: to pursue and catch Moon. Day after day, the dog tries every way he can to get the cat.

And Moon is on to him.

Whenever Charlie comes into the living room, the cat runs to the basement and hides. He doesn't emerge again until he's sure the dog has gone upstairs to the second floor.

Moon uses a secret entrance, a small hole next to the wall vent that leads down to the basement. Periodically the cat will come up from the basement, stick its head through the hole, and look around for Charlie. If the coast is clear, Moon can come out and enjoy life with the family.

On the other hand, if Charlie happens to be watching TV when Moon sticks his head out, the dog immediately jumps up and races furiously to the wall vent.

The cat ducks back inside, leaving the dog to slam into the wall and fall flat on the floor.

Charlie usually spends a few minutes lying there, trying to get his wits back; then he trots back to the couch.

One day two friends, who had expressed reservations about this strange teaching called Eckankar, came over to visit the family, who are ECKists. While they were chatting with their guests, Charlie sat with

Charlie is a dog, and Moon is a cat. Charlie's waking hours are devoted to one goal: to pursue and catch Moon.

them, one eye on the TV and the other watching for Moon to come out of the wall vent.

The visitors had no way of knowing this, of course.

Suddenly Charlie jumped up, raced to the wall, slammed his head against the vent, bounced off, and fell down. After a few minutes, he got up and returned to his place in front of the TV.

The visitors glanced at each other but didn't say anything. They couldn't help noticing that the ECK couple hadn't even turned around to look at the dog.

The two couples and Charlie sat quietly watching TV. Again, the dog caught a glimpse of Moon. For the second time, the visitors watched him jump up, run to the wall, hit his head, fall flat, and lie there recovering. A few minutes later he came back to join them near the TV.

The third time it happened, one of the friends finally spoke up.

"I don't want to pry, but I have a question to ask you," he said. "Your dog keeps jumping up and running into the wall, and you don't even seem to notice." He hesitated for a moment before going on.

Then he asked, "Has this anything to do with Eckankar?"

The ECKists started to laugh.

Realizing how their dog's antics must look to the visitors, they filled them in on the fourth member of their family, Moon the cat, who was trying to come out of hiding. "Every time Moon sticks his head out," they explained, "the dog takes off after him. By the time you look over there to see what's going on, the cat is out of sight again."

This simple explanation for Charlie's odd behavior made them realize the ECKists were really quite normal. With the deep, dark mystery gone, they lost their fear of Eckankar.

Our relationship with animals is often defined by what we most need to learn. Pets can teach us a great many things—patience, flexibility, how to live in the moment, how to laugh at ourselves. But most of all they can teach us how to give and receive unconditional love.

If there is something we really need to learn, a pet will sometimes be the instrument used by Divine Spirit to help us learn it.

Our relationship with animals is often defined by what we most need to learn.

The Two Little Hamsters

A family had a big black cat named Lucky. Lucky was a very good hunter. Some mornings when the mother opened the front door, the cat would be there with part of a mouse as a gift of love.

One weekend the family decided to go camping. In the children's room were a couple of hamsters who were family pets. The mother shut their bedroom door tightly; she wanted to be sure Lucky couldn't get into the room while they were gone and eat the hamsters.

When they were getting in the car, they couldn't find the black cat. Since this often happened before a trip, nobody worried about it.

Two days later when they got home, they heard meowing coming from the children's room.

The mother heard the sound and realized what had happened. Instead of protecting the hamsters by locking Lucky out of the bedroom, she had shut the cat in.

Instead of protecting the hamsters by locking Lucky out of the bedroom, she had shut the cat in.

She didn't have the courage to go and open the door herself. But her young children bolted for the door and threw it open.

The hamsters were alive and in good health.

And the big black cat was just sitting there quietly, very hungry from the two days without food.

The family had given so much love to the cat, and the cat had seen the love the family gave to the pet hamsters. Lucky knew they were pets and not food, that they too were part of the family.

Animals generally find it easy to see humans for what they are—Soul in another bodily form. We have a harder time with this. We want to be God's special creation, forgetting that, as Soul, we already are. And so also are animals.

Pretty Birds

*I*n winter, a woman liked to put out old bread and cereal for the birds and squirrels. The birds came from all around.

When she first started putting out food for the birds, the woman would shoo away crows and other not-so-pretty birds. If she was going to put out food, it ought to be for pretty birds.

But that month she had read her Eckankar discourse, a monthly letter I send to members of Eckankar. It contains spiritual instruction to assist them in their study. In this particular discourse, I suggested they do something purely for love without expecting anyone to say, "Thanks a lot for what you did; I appreciate it."

After she read the discourse, the woman decided she would try this as she fed the birds and animals.

So she put out the food. But no pretty birds came. Birds usually flock to her feeder from all around. But that day all that visited her were a squirrel and a crow.

The woman remembered the discourse and decided she would feed anything that came to her feeder. She would put out food for any bird or animal that came—and do it just for love.

As the days went by, the woman began to accept all birds and animals coming to the feeding station in her yard.

And with that change, love began to fill her heart.

As we unfold spiritually, we start to see how God's love sustains all things. We couldn't exist without it. We also begin to see the beauty that lies beneath the surface in other people, once we learn to open our hearts.

Misha

A woman had a Siamese cat, Misha, who always wanted love more than food.

One day the woman got a mate for Misha and called her Bani. Bani means Sound Current, the audible aspect of the Holy Spirit. And after a little while, Bani was going to have kittens.

On the day the kittens were to be born, Misha, the father, wanted to be in the room. But the woman said, "No, Misha, you stay out."

So Misha stayed outside the room.

Three Siamese kittens were born that day, and afterward the woman let Misha back in to be with them.

Misha began to sit guard outside the box. He'd watch over the kittens, he'd lick them, he'd take good care of them.

Mother cats have an instinct not to leave the kittens too long in one place because some predator might find them. Whenever Bani began to move the kittens, Misha would help. He'd hold one of the kittens by the scruff of the neck and very gently follow Bani.

A day came that the woman needed to leave on a trip, and she asked her niece to come over and take care of the cats. She had mentioned her trip to the veterinarian, and the vet said, "If you're going to be gone any length of time, it might be a good idea not

On the day the kittens were to be born, Misha, the father, wanted to be in the room. But the woman said, "No, Misha, you stay out."

to have the father cat in the room with the kittens. Sometimes the male cat will kill the kittens out of jealousy."

The woman didn't think Misha would do that, but she was going to be gone for a couple of days and thought it might be a good idea anyway.

So Bani and the three little kittens were in one room, and out in the hallway behind the shut door was Misha. Misha wanted to come in, but he couldn't.

The woman's niece was sitting in the room with Bani and the kittens. She suddenly saw kitty toys being pushed under the door.

Misha was pushing the toys under the door so Bani would have something to play with.

Misha was pushing the toys under the door so Bani would have something to play with.

When the woman was home again, she began wondering, "Are five Siamese cats too many?" So when a lady came by, she let her choose a kitten and take it to her mother. The family was astounded by the amount of love in this kitten. And pretty soon the lady called again.

Was it possible to get one of the remaining kittens for her husband and herself?

When the lady had first met Misha, on her previous visit, she was impressed by the love that was coming from him. She had said, "That cat has soul." She was trying to say, "That cat is a highly developed Soul."

Now when the couple came by and the lady saw Misha again, she said, "You have something very special with those cats of yours. There is so much love, and it's evident in your kittens."

Often when we speak of love, we think of it being exclusive to the human race. Yet if you have pets, you know that sometimes animals are capable of giving more of God's love than many humans can.

The Three Budgies

A couple from Sweden has a family of three budgies—little parakeets, Australian parrot-type birds. The three budgies each have a distinct personality.

Number one is Oscar. He's the chief, a nice green bird. Oscar is a very bluff fellow. He blusters and makes a big show of his self-importance. When he's confident, he fluffs his feathers up and makes himself real big.

But Oscar has another side. He's also a very fearful bird, afraid of the dark. He'd rather have light around him.

And Oscar likes music, but he's also a little stupid and clumsy.

The only female in this family of budgies is Gullen. She's a very shy bird unless the topic of food comes up. When it's mealtime, she's right there, and the other two birds scatter if they value their feathers.

Gullen also likes to sit exactly where one of the other birds is sitting. The birds may be loose in the room, one sitting on the couch. Gullen will go over and start taking the feathers out of the bird sitting on the couch. That bird leaves, and Gullen sits there, quite pleased and contented.

Generally Gullen is in the background, watching, but if people neglect her too long, she goes inside herself. And it takes much loving and coaxing to bring her out.

The third little bird is Chico. Greenish-blue or turquoise, he's the most social and highly intelligent. He's a newcomer. He had a previous owner.

Oscar and Gullen are a couple, and Chico is on the outside of the circle, so he's more sociable.

Oscar and Gullen are a couple, and Chico is on the outside of the circle, so he's more sociable. He has to be more sociable. Chico can also do something the other birds can't. Chico can talk.

When he came to his new owners, he'd say things like, "Washing machine," just out of the blue. Then he'd say, "Skating." His new owners were puzzled. What was this bird talking about? They really wondered when he said, "Whiskey"! Chico has been places, seen things, and done things. He is a bird of the world.

Chico even likes to clean, trim, and groom the mustache and beard of his owner. He likes everybody. Sometimes he puts his little beak out for a kiss. Since he's the only one who can talk or imitate, he goes around the room and chatters.

He will see Oscar and say, "Kiss, kiss?"

Oscar always looks rather puzzled; he doesn't know what to make of Chico. Oscar can't talk, and anyway, he is the chief. So what's this "kiss, kiss"?

An example of puzzled love. Oscar doesn't get it.

So Chico tries it with Gullen, the female. He puts a big smile on his little beak and says, "Kiss, kiss?" Gullen chases him away. She will have none of that from him, a bird of the world. Spurned love.

At night Chico goes to the top of the cage and, looking in the mirror, says, "Good night, Chico. Chico sweet. Kiss, kiss?"

At night, when it is time for all the good little birdies to say good night to the day, Chico goes to the top of the cage and stands on a perch in front of a mirror. He stands there, looking in the mirror, and says, "Good night, Chico. Chico sweet. Kiss, kiss?" It's lonely at the top.

Way down at the bottom of the cage, Oscar is on his perch, trying to get some sleep. Chico keeps talking and talking on into the night. Oscar looks up, ruffles his feathers, and stares at Chico, but it doesn't do any good because Chico is always looking in the mirror.

Oscar pulls himself together—because the chief has duties—and begins his slow, laborious way up the cage. Finally he gets to where Chico is, puffs himself real big, and stares down into the eyes of little Chico.

Then Chico makes himself small, stares back, and does not talk anymore.

Oscar, still in his enlarged state, makes his way back to his perch, sits down on it, and looks up very satisfied. He has done a good thing. The chief's duties are done for the day, and now all in his little village can rest.

The owner is always watching the three little birds, and in the meantime all the little lessons of love are rubbing off on him.

He and his wife do their spiritual exercises each evening by chanting *HU*, the beautiful love song to God. They sing it very quietly, and Chico always joins them. Oscar sits behind the sofa on a picture, listening. The birds know and recognize the sound of HU just like their human family.

Pets are carriers of God's love.

When you get into a relationship, you learn a lot about love. But you would do well to remember that the pets in our lives are also carriers of God's love.

Some of God's highest, most love-filled creatures exist in the animal world. Pets are Soul in another bodily form.

41

Where Have All the Turtles Gone?

*V*alerie left cold Illinois one November to visit a retired friend in Florida. A small pond graces his backyard.

He complained to her that his pond, once home to thirty-five turtles, now had no turtles at all. "Where have all the turtles gone?" he asked on several occasions.

A couple of weeks into the visit, he suggested a bike ride along the harbor and the lake, where they had ridden the previous year. This bike path ends near a busy road. There, Valerie suddenly felt a presence. Only fifteen feet from the road sat a very large turtle, which let her approach without any sign of fear.

Then a picture from the past flashed through her mind.

She knew this turtle. They'd met the previous year, after a car had run over it, cracking its shell and leaving it on the road with serious injuries. Valerie had gently moved it out of harm's way, setting it in some grass. At her initial touch, the turtle had panicked. But she softly sang *HU*, the ancient love song to God, which soothed its fearful struggling.

So the turtle now recognized her. It was a meeting between two old friends.

But the road was still a dangerous place for a turtle. Valerie picked up her fifty-pound friend,

A picture from the past flashed through her mind. She knew this turtle.

43

bicycled with this enormous load under her arm through a park amid unbelieving stares, and took it to her friend's place. The next day, Valerie also found its mate and reunited them. Both soon had a new home in the backyard pond. A much safer place for breeding turtles.

Twice now, God's love showed itself to her turtle friend through her acts of kindness.

A Spiritual Exercise to Find Love

*E*veryone is looking for love. So how do you find it?

As a spiritual exercise, you can say, "Dear God, teach me how to love." If you ask this of the divine power with sincerity, with a desire to know truth, I can guarantee you that your life will change in very dramatic ways.

But remember that divine love is a two-way thing. It flows to us from God, and when it comes to us, we as Soul must also give it back in some way to someone else.

This is the nature of life.

CHAPTER THREE

Animals Can Be Our Teachers

Pappagena Finds Freedom

A woman had a cockatiel named Pappagena. One day the bird was sitting outside his cage—singing, pecking at seeds, and having a good time.

By some fluke, the wind blew the front door open, and the woman jumped up to close it before Pappagena could get out. But her abrupt movement startled the bird.

Pappagena took off, flying right out the door.

The woman ran outside after the bird. She saw him rise higher and higher, soon to disappear among the trees.

"Pappagena!" she called out. "Pappagena, come home!" But the bird didn't come.

The woman ran back in the house and began calling all the usual sources of help—her mother, then the fire department. No one could figure out how to lure her cockatiel back home.

The distraught woman finally picked up the phone and dialed the Eckankar Spiritual Center in Minneapolis. A staff member, earnestly wanting to help, suggested she try a spiritual exercise.

The woman quickly hung up the phone, closed her eyes, and tried to visualize Wah Z, the Inner Master. She saw him cooing to the bird, "Come home now, Pappagena. Mommy's waiting for you."

She waited throughout the night, but Pappagena didn't come home.

The woman ran outside after the bird. She saw him rise higher and higher, soon to disappear among the trees.

Early the next morning, she went outside and called to the bird again. This time he answered her with a song, but still he remained hidden in the trees.

So she decided to do another spiritual exercise. This one was called the Shariyat technique, where you ask an inner question and open *The Shariyat-Ki-Sugmad,* a sacred book in Eckankar, at random.

"How can I get Pappagena to come home?" the woman asked and opened the book. The first passage she opened to spoke of freedom; the second talked of love.

Pappagena was her pet and she loved him, but the woman suddenly realized that she didn't own him. His true nature was Soul, manifested in this life as a bird. He needed freedom.

Pappagena had to decide whether or not to accept her love and the freedom her love could give him.

Could she love the bird and still allow him freedom? For his own safety, she had to keep him indoors; he was not a bird of prey. Yet Pappagena had to decide whether or not to accept her love and the freedom her love could give him.

She went outside and called Pappagena again. He sang out his answer from way up in a tree.

"I know you are Soul, I know you are free," she told him. "If you want to stay here with me, I will love you. But it's your choice. You can go now if you want to. It doesn't make any difference to me."

She was sincere. At this point, it really didn't make any difference to her. She went back in the house, totally released from her attachment to Pappagena.

Just as the day was turning to dusk, she heard a scratching on the window. She went out to the yard to look around, and the bird landed right on her head.

They are now living happily together again.

The woman had learned to let go, to truly let go. She respected and loved Pappagena as Soul. And because of this, she found love in return.

Until we see animals as Souls, we will miss much of what they have to teach us. Most of all, we'll miss the love. So many people today are seeking love, but they are looking for it mainly in human love. That is fine, so far as it goes. But there is more, much more to it.

The woman had learned to let go, to truly let go. She respected and loved Pappagena as Soul.

The Emperor Moth
Teaches a Hard Lesson

A biologist found the cocoon of an emperor moth and took it to his lab for study. *What a wonderful opportunity to watch this moth come out!* he thought. So the cocoon sat on his lab table for quite a while.

Finally it began to tremble as the moth made its efforts to come out into the world.

The scientist noticed that the cocoon was shaped like a bottle, wide at the bottom but very narrow at the top. The top was surrounded by a concretelike substance.

He watched the cocoon for a while, growing more and more impatient. How could the moth make it through that hard material? Finally he decided to help it out. Using a tiny pair of scissors, he carefully cut through the concretelike rim at the top of the cocoon.

How could the moth make it through that hard material? Finally he decided to help it out.

The moth popped out almost instantly.

The biologist waited for the moth to spread its beautiful wings and show its pretty colors. But nothing happened. The moth was misshapen, with a huge body and very tiny wings. He watched it walk around slowly, unable to lift itself off the table. Eventually it died, never having flown.

As the scientist began to read about the emperor moth, trying to figure out what had happened, he found that other biologists had made the same mis-

53

take he had. They, too, had tried to ease the moth's difficult entry into the world by cutting the lip of the cocoon. And they had discovered the purpose for the cocoon being wide at the bottom with a narrow neck and a very tight top.

As the moth forces itself through the narrow neck of the cocoon, it must streamline its body. The fluids in its body are squeezed into the wings. This process makes the wings large and the body small. When it finally emerges into the world, the emperor moth is a creature unsurpassed in its beauty.

The biologist realized he had actually done the moth a disservice by sparing it what he thought to be unnecessary hardship. Deprived of its natural birthing process, the moth had emerged a misshapen creature, incapable of fulfilling its potential.

It might seem like an apparent contradiction that the emperor moth must go through such a slow, intense struggle to get out of its cocoon in order to be born into the world as a beautiful creature. Yet it's not unlike the spiritual life.

Quite often people approach the MAHANTA, the Living ECK Master to complain about their hardships. "Why is my life so difficult?" they'll ask. "Why can't you take this burden away from me?" The problems generally fall into three major categories: health, finances, and love. If the problem isn't resolved quickly enough for them, they'll ask, "Haven't you any power?"

They don't realize that intervention at the wrong time, or too soon, can create a misshapen form not properly prepared to reach the high worlds of God.

Life will give us many lessons to help us learn the Law of Noninterference, to step back and let others have the experiences they need to grow spiritually.

Quite often it is the only way they can acquire the inner strength they need to take the next step on their journey home to God.

Life will give us many lessons to help us learn.

It's a Bald Rooster, Don't Laugh

On a farm in Africa, a hen laid a bunch of eggs that were fertilized by a funny-looking rooster whose head and neck were bald.

Every time the rooster walked into the yard, the family would laugh and laugh.

It was all pretty funny until the eggs hatched. One of the chicks came out looking exactly like the rooster—bald head, bald neck. Because the little thing was so ugly and small, the other chicks picked on it and even broke its leg. To protect it, the family had to bring it into the house.

One member of the family wrote me a letter about this. He had a very interesting observation: "We laughed at this rooster that was bald-headed and bald-necked, and now all of a sudden we find that one just like him has taken up residence in our home!"

Thoughts of any nature come home to roost. This is called the Law of Karma, or the Law of Cause and Effect. We reap what we sow.

The same laws of life that apply to nature and animals apply to us. These are the laws of Divine Spirit, the subtle principles of life which hold everything together.

The better we understand these laws, the easier our life will be.

Thoughts of any nature come home to roost.

Cows on Ice,
a Lot like People

*B*ack in 1932 during the Depression, a boy and his family moved from Iowa to the Thief River Falls area of Minnesota. On March 1 of that year, the temperature was minus thirty-three degrees.

The family had a herd of thirty cows, and the cows were mostly kept inside. The river froze, so the father and son went down to the river and cut a hole in the ice, about thirty feet out, to let the cows drink.

The father and son cut a hole in the ice, thirty feet out, to let the cows drink.

The boy's job was to take the cattle down to the river every day. The herd would come down the bank, walk across the ice to the water hole, and drink. Then the boy would take the cows back up to the barn.

This all went very nicely until spring came. Then the ice began to thaw.

The ice near the bank began to thaw first. Each day the cows would stand on the bank, looking at their water hole thirty feet out on the ice. Then they would walk through two feet of water, climb back on the ice, walk across the ice, and drink out of the hole. When it was time to go back to the barn, they would walk back across the ice, wade through two feet of water, and climb back up on the bank.

This went on for days.

The boy couldn't believe it. These cows had to drink out of the same water hole, even though they practically drowned getting to it. And as the weather warmed, more of the ice thawed, the water got deeper, and the trek became riskier.

You can almost hear the cows walking through the water. "Boy, this stuff is cold!" they're saying to each other. "Why isn't it like before, when we could just walk out there and not have to go through this cold stuff?"

One day, when the cows got to the river they saw that their water hole had sailed downstream.

One day, when the cows got to the river they saw that their water hole had sailed downstream, never to be seen again. Finally, they looked down at their feet and began to drink the water that was there.

It's easy for us to laugh at dumb cows. People aren't like that. But sometimes people are very much like that. Sometimes people have a habit of drinking from a water hole thirty feet off the riverbank, across the ice, because it's what they've always done. And they insist on going there long after there is any need to do it. That is the nature of habits.

Quite often, the main thing holding us back from greater spiritual growth is a fixed state of mind. Even after a habit has shown itself to be of no further use to us, we hang on to it anyway.

Out of habit, I guess.

Is Sugarbear
Losing Her Mind?

My daughter's friend had a little dog named Sugarbear. Everyone picked on Sugarbear—other dogs, cats, even kittens.

In due time, Sugarbear began to show some strange behavior. She would run out into the middle of the road, spray a little, then sit down. Cars would stop, honk, and slowly drive around her.

My daughter and her friend wondered, *Is Sugarbear losing her mind?* Maybe the world had beaten up on her so much that it had affected her reason.

One day my daughter saw a cat walk up to the house, spray a bush to mark his territory, then walk away. Pretty soon a dog came walking up, sniffed at the bush, and sprayed it too. He had recaptured the territory for his own. Finally a little kitten came along after the dog and marked the bush for herself.

About this time, Sugarbear came out of the house. She sniffed the bush and realized that it had already been claimed by some greater power. So she ran into the middle of the road and marked her territory out there.

Sugarbear came out of the house. She ran into the middle of the road and marked her territory out there.

Nobody else wanted that territory; thus she didn't have a lot of competition.

People sometimes wonder why the explorers of old got in their little boats and went sailing off into the unknown. There were significant dangers involved and not many creature comforts. But they were like little Sugarbear going out in the middle of the road. They needed freedom, and they couldn't find it in the towns and settlements. So they went where no one else had the courage to go.

The sincere seeker of God is just like Sugarbear. One day he says, "I want freedom" and sets off to find it.

This means having the courage to venture into new areas of consciousness, to let the Light and Sound of God work with you. This alone will bring about the changes needed for Self-Realization, true awareness of yourself as Soul.

The Ant and the Feather— a Lesson on Fear

A woman lived in California. English was her second language, and she wasn't very comfortable with it. Even though she did very well in business and wrote fluently, she felt her speech was choppy. She would get the English sentence structure backward, and sometimes she came across as too abrupt.

Every Tuesday this woman was one of the leaders at a management group. Her language skills often got in the way.

She began to dread Tuesdays. Sometimes she was able to pull it off, but other days she was reduced to tears afterward as she drove home.

One day the woman went out for a walk. She was crying. "MAHANTA, please help me overcome this problem that I have," she said. "Help me with this fear."

In front of her there was a hill. She heard a silent nudge, the silent voice from the Inner Master, the MAHANTA: "Go to the top of the hill." So she walked up the hill, and she saw the clouds. They were blue and pink, very pretty and wispy.

By the time she got to the top of the hill where the wind was blowing, much of the burden had lifted from her. She felt happier.

She looked down at her feet and saw an ant. The ant was pulling on a feather about thirty times larger than itself. The feather was a huge burden for

The feather was a huge burden for the little ant. It was trying to pull the feather into the wind.

the little ant. It was trying to pull the feather into the wind.

Why does the ant bother? the woman thought. *It's not food. Where is the anthill? Where would the ant possibly want to take this feather?* You can imagine an ant coming home with this huge feather, and the mother ant saying, "You're not bringing that thing in the house!"

She watched the ant struggle and struggle.

Finally, the ant stopped. It let go of the feather, and the feather blew away. The ant scurried off looking a lot freer and happier.

She realized her fear was like that feather. If she could let go and let love enter into her life, love would displace the fear.

As the woman watched this, she realized her fear was just like that feather. If she could let go and let love enter into her life, love would displace the fear, and the fear would no longer have any power over her.

It's interesting that the image Divine Spirit brought to her in this waking dream was a feather. What's a feather? It's a plume. Something to say, "Look what a dandy I am!" It was a feather in the cap of the ant, so he thought, to come home with this beautiful thing. Wouldn't everyone envy him! But the feather was really a burden, like the woman's fear.

To let go of fear, we allow divine love to flow in and take its place. The woman had already done this with her smaller fears. Now, thanks to a tiny ant, she had learned to do it with a big fear.

A Horse's Look of Love
Heals the Heart

A woman from Trinidad felt as if her life had gone to hell in a handbasket. Her marriage had just broken up. Then her son began using drugs.

Life was pretty hard, so much so that one day, while she was driving to work, tears began pouring down the woman's cheeks. She decided to pull the car off the road and just cry.

She pulled up beside a field where young horses were grazing. Still crying, she got out of the car to enjoy their beauty.

Suddenly one of the horses stopped what he was doing and came galloping toward her. He came right up to the fence where she was standing. Then he raised his head and looked directly into her eyes.

An incredible stream of love flowed from the horse to her.

Once the woman understood the gift of love had been passed to her, the horse shook his head, snorted, and trotted back to the rest of the herd.

Animals had often been a means Divine Spirit used to bring love to this woman. She recognized this was the blessing of the Holy Spirit bringing comfort to her. It was a gift from the MAHANTA.

The woman further realized there is no need to *speak* love with people, animals, or plants, but just

One of the horses came up to the fence where she was standing.

be love. If you are love, then the person or animal you love will know.

Scruffy the Squirrel Learns a Lesson on Karma

A woman had a plot in a community garden in her neighborhood. Each plot measured about five by eight feet. She planted all sorts of vegetables in her plot—lettuce, kale, broccoli, carrots, and cucumbers—everything she could think of. She loved her little garden, every square inch of it.

As gardeners do, the woman soon became acquainted with the squirrels. One of them she named Scruffy because he had a patch of fur missing from his head and another missing from his back. What's more, his tail was stripped, as if someone had singed it.

She noticed that Scruffy was a tough little squirrel, despite his appearance. Nobody messed with him.

The woman was concerned that the squirrels would eat her vegetables. So she made a silent agreement with them: "I'll bring you snacks every day if you leave my garden alone."

Squirrels are very intelligent. Apparently they understood. Every day she would arrive with a grocery bag, and the squirrels would gather around. Scruffy would do a little act for her. He'd run around in circles, do tricks, then go into a classic pose—one hand over his heart and the other held out for food.

Then the woman would reach into her bag for peanuts. This went on day after day.

Next to her garden was a plot belonging to a group of schoolchildren. Their teachers would bring them to the garden and let them plant whatever they wanted. The children had little interest in the garden; it took work, and the plants grew slowly. So the woman took it upon herself to water their garden too, and it came along very nicely.

One day she noticed a bare spot in the corner of her garden. At the same time she saw there were some healthy-looking collard greens in the children's plot.

"I'm owed something for watering their garden," she said to herself. "Otherwise, all they'd have is brown dirt."

She went over to the children's garden and very carefully dug up three tiny collard plants. After all, she reasoned, the children would never miss them. She put the three collard plants in her own garden, in the bare spot.

Time went by, and the woman's garden grew. Her cucumber vine was especially healthy. It had three little cucumbers, just about ready to pick. "Pretty soon," she said, "I'm going to have a nice salad with those cucumbers. I'll invite a friend over, and we'll have a good time."

A few days later, she came to the garden to harvest the three cucumbers. But when she got to her plot, the plant was bare. Not one cucumber remained!

The woman was very upset. She went around to the other gardeners and asked them, "Do you know what happened to my cucumbers?" They all said they had no idea. She went back to her little garden, still fuming.

Scruffy came up to her, stood there for a moment, then went into his little act. He did all his usual tricks, chased his tail for a while, then assumed his classic beggar's pose.

She glared at him. "Scruffy, what do you know about these cucumbers?"

Scruffy held his pose for a few seconds, then under her withering gaze, he melted. He ran over to the children's plot and stood there, chattering at her. The woman walked over.

In the very spot where she had dug up the children's collard greens lay two of her cucumbers, half eaten.

Then Scruffy ran back to her plot and stood near a far corner. She walked over, and there was the third cucumber. It, too, was half eaten.

The woman began to laugh. She could suddenly see the divine justice in all of this. She knew she had no right to take someone else's property, even if she had taken care of their garden. It was God's way of telling her, in a loving and gentle manner, "You've got to respect other people's property or you stand to lose your own."

She realized she'd encroached upon the property of the children. And when she had, Divine Spirit sent her a message in the form of Scruffy, the sassy little squirrel, to remind her once again of this law of balance, the Law of Karma. It's what the Bible states as, "Whatsoever a man soweth, that shall he also reap."

The woman's lesson from Scruffy the squirrel was simple too: learn to love and respect your neighbor, as much as you love and respect yourself.

She could suddenly see the divine justice in all of this. It was God's way of telling her, "You've got to respect other people's property or you stand to lose your own."

A Llama's Warning Cry

A man and his wife owned a farm in the eastern part of the United States. They had llamas and sheep, and outside the fence they had coyotes.

The coyotes spent their time trying to figure out if it was worth it to go inside the fence to get the sheep. But inside the fence was also where the llamas were. And llamas are very protective of sheep.

A llama has a very peculiar warning cry. It sounds like a siren. The first time the man heard this siren sound, he had no idea what was going on. He ran outside, prepared for just about anything.

It was the llama sending a warning to a coyote or some other animal that was thinking about coming after the flock of sheep.

You have to consider that Divine Spirit, the Holy Spirit, watches out for each of you, for your safety and spiritual well-being, with as much care as a llama looks after the sheep in its care.

The Holy Spirit, or the ECK, is a wave which comes from God, made up of both the Light and the Sound. It is the Voice of God, the Sound Current.

It speaks to us in different ways. Sometimes it's through intuition, sometimes through a messenger speaking for the spiritual hierarchy, like a guardian angel. It also speaks to us through dreams.

Llamas are interesting, and the Holy Spirit is interesting too.

Divine Spirit watches out for each of you, for your safety and spiritual well-being, with as much care as a llama looks after the sheep in its care.

A Spiritual Exercise
for Protection

*I*f you sing *HU*, a holy name for God, you will find that It opens your heart to the guidance of Divine Spirit.

Little by little, you will become better able to discern the gentle inner voice of the MAHANTA. The MAHANTA is an expression of the ECK, the Holy Spirit, in a form people can understand. This inner voice, like a silent nudge, will show you how to live your life better.

And should you ever be in danger, this inner voice will sound a warning. It will warn you in times of danger and throw a mantle of protection around you.

When you practice singing *HU* every day, the ECK, the Holy Spirit, will watch out for you.

CHAPTER FOUR

Animals Are Learning Too

Lucky the Squirrel

*T*he window at my writing desk looks out into our backyard, which borders a small grove of trees. My wife and I call it "the forest."

This forest is home to our family of animals: a chipmunk, some red foxes that drop by in search of a meal, Mr. and Mrs. Rabbit, and a tree full of squirrels. All of them, even the foxes at times, come to eat birdseed from two feeding dishes set out for them.

The squirrels are the most fun to watch. Two large squirrels hog the feeding dishes by sitting down in them, chasing away lesser members of the family who must get by with old seed on the ground. After eating, the family retires to the forest to relax and play.

Yet life is not a paradise. To spoil this happy scene, a neighbor's brown-and-white dog races by on occasion to chase the birds and animals at the dishes. But they always manage to flee in time.

One day I saw a newcomer to our family: a small rabbit with short ears. He ate from the dish of birdseed then hopped toward a tall tree in the forest. Idly, I watched. To my surprise, he didn't run around the tree like a normal rabbit.

Instead, he ran straight up the trunk. What a marvelous trick!

After watching for a while, I realized he wasn't a rabbit at all. He was a squirrel who'd traded his tail for his life, much to the chagrin of his pursuer.

One day I saw a newcomer to our family: a small rabbit with short ears.

We began to call the tailless squirrel Lucky.

He was a squirrel who'd traded his tail for his life.

Many people in pursuit of God are like the birds and animals in our backyard. In fact, they are like Lucky. Gorging on food and drink, they trip off to play in the forest, returning to the feeding dish each day for more of the same. And life rolls merrily on. Then one day, a complication comes to steal a prized possession, like Lucky's handsome tail.

And life is nevermore the same. But it goes on.

Molly and the
Great Unmovable

*F*or years my wife and I shared our home with a little dog named Molly. Eventually she lost her sight and hearing, but she was still filled with love—and she was still every bit as stubborn as a puppy.

Molly's goal was to understand the Great Unmovable, which happened to be our library bookcase. We had set up a protected area in the living room where she could walk around. The walls were foam padded, but the front of the bookcase was not. Yet Molly toddled along so slowly that she really couldn't hurt herself.

As soon as she got up from her bed, she headed straight to the bookcase, and for some reason she proceeded to press against it with all her might. We were not sure whether she wanted to shove it over or if she was trying to absorb all the wisdom she could from the books.

Her technique was to position her head against the front of the bookcase and push at it until she couldn't push anymore. Then she just stood there like a bull with his head against a wall.

But she was not ready to give up yet.

Walking around to the little space at the side of the bookcase, she'd brace herself against the wall and press her head against the enemy. Then she'd push and push until she was practically standing on her

She headed straight to the bookcase and proceeded to press against it with all her might.

head and rolled over on her side.

Every time Molly fell over, she got right up and began to walk around in tight little circles, just as we do when we're trying to get a mental grasp on something beyond our comprehension. Once she got her bearings again, she lined up for the next attack.

Molly's lesson was to learn how to back up.

We all have lessons to learn in life. It's better to work smarter, not harder. I think Molly's lesson in this lifetime was to learn how to back up. My wife and I can't remember a time when she ever did. I don't think it was in her to do it.

Since animals are Souls, they too are learning spiritual lessons. They too are on the journey home to God.

The Hideous God

*I*t's always very lively at our backyard bird feeder. My wife and I enjoy watching our family—the birds and other creatures who come.

All they know is that the dish is always full. They don't know who their God is, who provides the food.

It snowed early this year, and a pheasant joined the group at the feeder. When the pheasant runs, he looks like a cartoon character: he puts his head up, goes "Ock!" then shoots away. The pheasant is stealthy. He comes through his little patch of wood very quietly and carefully. Usually the red and gray squirrels, the rabbits, and the other wildlife are at the feeding dish, but they don't notice the pheasant because of his camouflage.

Then he gives this terrible honk. The rabbits jump straight up in the air, and the squirrels dash off. Pretty soon the area is cleared, and the pheasant can walk up and eat.

One day, I was working and remembered it was time to feed the birds and animals. I went to the back door where the feed is stored and opened it. A winter rabbit and a gray squirrel were very startled; they acted as if they had seen the great monster from the other side.

When I came back in, I told my wife, "I think I am their hideous God."

Paul Twitchell wrote about the hideous God in *The Tiger's Fang*. Some of you may have read this book

This year, a pheasant joined the group at the feeder.

81

about the spiritual journey that Paul Twitchell made to God Consciousness.

To a pheasant, I suppose God looks like another pheasant, except bigger. The pheasant prays to his pheasant God, the great blessed winged father of all pheasants. Then one day he sees me putting out the food, and he can't believe his eyes.

He runs off ten steps, then stops and turns to look one more time. "Yup. Ugly as I thought," he probably says, then runs off.

The birds and animals at our feeder get their food from their hideous God who stands behind this curtain. They never see him. They couldn't stand the shock; they couldn't separate the gift from the giver, except to say, "The gift is good, and the giver is hideous."

Often people are like these birds and animals out in the backyard. They pray to God, they praise God, and they thank God for the food and bountiful blessings. They have their notions about God too. They put together some human characteristics they admire, some noble traits and qualities, and say this is God, the great God of all goodness.

But if God were ever to show his face, or her face, or its face—whatever they believe God to be—they would practically fall over from sheer fright. Because they never imagined their God could be so hideous.

If God ever showed Itself to people, how many could stand the sight of God, in God's true glory?

To a pheasant, I suppose God looks like another pheasant, except bigger.

Shredded Wheat

*S*hredded wheat was once my wife's special cereal. She'd eat it a lot, with fruit and other things on it. She just loved it.

One day I ran out of birdseed. "I don't know what to do until tomorrow when the store's open," I told my wife.

"If you want to give them some of my shredded wheat, you can," she said. So I filled two bowls with shredded wheat and carried them outside to the feeding area.

A couple of hours later we looked out the window; the dishes were still full. There were plenty of tracks in the snow leading up to the shredded wheat, but nobody had touched it. The next morning it was still there, and there were a lot more tracks. So I went to the store and bought some birdseed.

There were plenty of tracks in the snow leading up to the shredded wheat, but nobody had touched it.

After that I noticed my wife didn't eat her special cereal as often. She figured that if the birds and animals won't touch it, maybe there isn't much value in it. Some very wise beings in the neighborhood had tested it and didn't give it their stamp of approval.

You learn from nature. Sometimes the lessons you learn are very good ones, but they can catch you totally off guard.

The Basket of Acorns

One day I was having lunch with a few of the ECK Initiates who work at the Temple of ECK. They brought me a very special gift.

They had gone to the woods on the Temple grounds, and underneath a red oak tree they found some fallen acorns. After gathering up a bunch of them, they very carefully washed them off and placed them in a nice little basket. They handed this to me over lunch.

"That's very kind of you," I said. "I think I'll have one."

"We brought them for your squirrels," they said.

"We brought them for your squirrels," they said.

"I don't think you want to eat them," one of the ECKists added. When somebody tells you that, of course, you have to do it anyway.

I went home and tried to remember how we used to open hickory nuts when I was a kid. We would store them in a milk can in the garage loft for half the winter. Once the nuts were dried out, my brothers and I would climb up the ladder and fill our pockets. Then we'd take them to the barn, lay them out on the floor, and crush them with our heels.

I did the same with one of the acorns, then put some of the fruit in my mouth. It was the bitterest thing I'd ever tasted. The ECKist who warned me against eating them knew what she was talking about. She had probably tried some herself.

When it was time to feed the squirrels, I took the birdseed outside and poured it into their two dishes, then put a little bit extra on the patio for the birds. Curious to see how our squirrels would deal with the acorns, I dropped a handful into each of the dishes.

I went in the house and stood by the window to watch. The first squirrel approached the dish, cautiously picked up an acorn, and went absolutely crazy. He jumped up and down, ran around in a circle, then tore off across the lawn.

Up in the trees the other squirrels, noticing all the commotion down there, had to see what was going on. They ran down and found the acorns, then promptly went crazy too.

They each took an acorn and scurried across the lawn in a different direction.

I had always heard that squirrels are very industrious, burying the acorns so that they would have food in the winter. Let me tell you, our squirrels will never find their acorns again. They have no idea where they put the things.

They ran back to the dishes several times for more acorns, which they carried around for a while before dropping them in the grass. They didn't even dig holes. When they'd emptied the dishes, they ran back out on the lawn and tried to find them.

In the twenty minutes I watched, only one squirrel found one acorn, probably because he stubbed his toe on it.

We laugh at these little fellows running hither and thither with their precious load, hiding it and then failing to find it later. Yet this is pretty much how it is with the human consciousness too.

We find something of spiritual value and say, "Hey, look at this." Then we store it away, hoping to use it later.

The first squirrel approached the dish, cautiously picked up an acorn, and went absolutely crazy.

But we forget we ever had it, and life goes on as it did before.

The day will come, however, perhaps in the dead of winter, when we think, *Whatever happened to those wonderful morsels I found last summer? I really need them now.*

Quite often we learn more about spirituality in the winter of life, when times are hard, than during the summer when times are easy.

Animals, birds, and people are pretty much alike, because we're all Soul.

Animals, birds, and people are pretty much alike, because we're all Soul.

The Hen Who
Ate the Rice

*O*ne day a man who lives in Nigeria went to visit a friend in town. Returning home, he stood by himself at the bus stop on a very busy highway filled with vehicles of all kinds.

Just then a pickup truck loaded with bags of rice came along. As it passed, the truck hit an enormous bump. Some rice, spilled into the truck bed, flew up into the air and fell on the highway.

In the brush by the road were five birds. Two were just ordinary birds, but three were chickens. Somehow these hens knew some rice had fallen on the highway.

All three rushed into the road, trying to get to the spilled rice.

The first cars that drove by frightened them. With a cackle the hens all ran back into the brush, and the other birds flew away.

Only one hen came back.

This hen looked at the rice with one eye, and with the other eye she looked at the traffic coming down the road. She weighed her chances, and she ran right out into the road again.

The cars were coming fast. With one eye on the vehicles and the other eye on the grain, the hen ate a little bit here, a little bit there, dodging in and around all the vehicles. Finally, after fifty cars and

This hen looked at the rice with one eye, and with the other eye she looked at the traffic coming down the road. She weighed her chances.

trucks had missed her, she finished eating and ran back to the side of the road, very satisfied with herself.

She cleaned her beak and went back into the brush where the others were still digging in the dirt for anything they could find. She had just had a feast.

The man looked at this hen and marveled at her daring spirit. The battle for survival is adventuresome and not a game for weaklings, he realized. To succeed one has to throw in all he or she has. Wit, skills, a daring spirit, and a heart full of love.

This daring hen had it all.

To succeed one has to throw in all he or she has. Wit, skills, a daring spirit, and a heart full of love.

The Electric Fence

*A*t home on the farm we had fences around the grain fields. At first we had ordinary wire fences; then Dad put up electric fences. It gave the cows a little less incentive to push through and eat the oats and corn in the next field.

Cows have personalities. There are the smart ones, and there are the not-so-smart ones. A not-so-smart cow would stand by a fence, chewing her cud, thinking of heaven knows what. The smart cows would be standing off to the side saying, "Little bit more to the left."

Cows have personalities. There are the smart ones, and there are the not-so-smart ones.

Suddenly one of the smart cows would run, head down, into the side of the stupid cow and knock the wind out of her. You could just hear the cow go, "Hoo-oo-oo!"

The smart cow would push the stupid cow through the electric fence, the stupid cow would get the shock, and the fence would fall down and short out.

Then the rest of the herd would walk through the fence into the field of oats or corn.

I noticed that even the most stupid cow got a little smarter after she hit the electric fence a few times. Often she still stood near it, but she wasn't chewing her cud as contentedly as before. She was looking around, watching the other cows.

We humans have to learn the same lesson—not to let other people push us through the fence. You

We have to learn the same lesson—not to let other people push us through the fence.

may, for example, know you can't handle sugar very well. Someone says, "Would you like some ice cream on your pie?" You have to know that pie alone or ice cream alone is OK, but the two together is like hitting the electric fence.

But sometimes the only way to learn a spiritual law is to run into the fence. Then we know.

A Spiritual Exercise
for Survival

*M*ost of our problems are caused because, spiritually, we cannot back up. We come up against something bigger than we are, and we say, "I'm going to beat this." Or we say, "I haven't tried as hard as I can."

But there is a better way. A way to go with the flow of ECK, the Holy Spirit.

The simplest way is to sing or chant *HU* whenever you come up against something that seems unmovable. If you can remember, stand back and sing this ancient love song to God, inwardly or outwardly, silently or softly. Then wait to see what comes through.

Divine Spirit will give you some insight on how to approach your problem from another angle.

If you sing *HU* every day for ten minutes, filling your heart with as much love as you can, you will find a greater awareness of the factors affecting your survival, both here on earth and on the inner planes.

CHAPTER FIVE

Contemplating with Animals

The Flock of Birds

*A*fter the ECK Worldwide Seminar one year, a woman wanted to share her experiences there with a friend back home. One Sunday they got together and went for a walk in a beautiful forest. As they walked, she began to tell her friend about all the love she'd experienced at the seminar.

They came to a clearing and found themselves on top of a cliff that rose out of the forest. A clear lake sparkled below; overhead, the sky was a brilliant blue. *What a perfect day,* the ECKist thought.

Turning to her friend she said, "In one of the workshops at the seminar, we were told that if we wanted to find divine love, we could chant *HU* quietly within ourselves. At the same time we could say, 'Show me love, MAHANTA. Show me love, MAHANTA.' This seems like a perfect time to do it."

And so, standing high atop a cliff overlooking the sparkling blue lake, the ECKist began to chant *HU*.

"Show me love, MAHANTA," she said silently. "Show me love, MAHANTA."

All of a sudden a small flock of birds came fluttering down. Some landed on the ground in front of her, while others perched in a nearby tree.

The Inner Master—the MAHANTA, the inner side of myself—nudged her, "Hold out your hand." She felt silly, but she put out her hand anyway. One little bird flew down from the tree and lit on it.

The Inner Master nudged her, "Hold out your hand." One little bird flew down and lit on it.

97

"This can't be," she said, laughing with joy. She felt the love of the ECK and the MAHANTA coming through the little bird. The love was so strong and pure she began to weep. She realized the ECK cared so much for her that It would show her Its love even through the humblest of Its creatures.

The two friends left the cliff and continued on their walk. About two hours later, they came back the same way. "I'm going to try it again," the woman said.

Silently she chanted *HU* and said, "Show me love, MAHANTA. Show me love." She almost couldn't believe it: another flock of birds flew down, she held out her hand, and once again, a little bird landed on it.

She knew then that the love of the ECK is real, the love of the ECK is truth. It is the Light and Sound of God, and It will show Itself through the humblest of Its creatures—if only we will be the humblest of Its creatures.

Maggie and Thor

An ECK Initiate was in the habit of doing her spiritual exercises each night in the living room. She would sit on the floor, her two large dogs nearby, then close her eyes and sing *HU*, the love song to God.

Fortunately, her dogs, Maggie and Thor, always sat quietly as she sang, "*HU-U-U-U.*" They didn't try to help by howling along. This could be quite a distraction, especially if the dogs weigh a hundred pounds each and have voices to match.

The woman's husband finally finished remodeling the attic, which he had made into their bedroom. It was such a pretty room, she decided this was where she'd now do the spiritual exercises.

The first night she and her dogs went up to her new attic bedroom, she noticed a peculiar thing. As soon as she sat down and began to sing *HU*, Thor and Maggie left the room. The same thing happened the next night and the next.

She couldn't understand why. The two dogs always followed her wherever she went and stayed right with her. But something had changed.

One night she went into her new bedroom and began the Spiritual Exercises of ECK to strengthen her connection with the inner worlds. Once again, as soon as she closed her eyes and started to sing *HU*, she heard Maggie and Thor run out of the room.

She would sit on the floor, her two large dogs nearby, then close her eyes and sing HU, *the love song to God.*

Am I singing HU *in the wrong key?* she wondered. *Did the dogs change their minds and decide they don't want to do the spiritual exercises anymore?*

One night she decided to find out what was going on. As usual, the dogs followed her upstairs to the bedroom. She began to sing *HU*, and the dogs dashed out of the room. This time she followed them.

They headed down the stairs and straight to the living room.

As she watched them get comfortable in their favorite spot and shut their eyes, she suddenly realized what was happening. Her chanting *HU* signaled the start of the spiritual exercises, and the dogs came down to their established place in the living room so they could do theirs too.

Many pets that come into the homes of ECKists are very high spiritual beings. They too know and appreciate the beauty of this love song to God, the HU.

The Parrot Who Sang *HU*

A family had a temperamental parrot. When the bird was in one of his bad moods, he would squawk and carry on, making all kinds of noise.

One day the owners decided that they couldn't put up with the parrot's bad habits anymore. He was becoming a real pest in the household.

"What if we chanted *HU*?" the husband asked.

They didn't try to change the parrot, but they knew singing *HU* would open the way for ECK, the Holy Spirit, to bring divine love into their household.

The next few times the parrot got noisy and disruptive, the owners chanted *HU*. The bird quickly quieted down and became very docile, and the household was once again peaceful. It even got to the point where the parrot joined in.

Some human beings think animals are so low on the scale of life that they could not possibly provide a suitable embodiment for Soul. But in Eckankar we know that animals are Souls.

And since they are Soul, they, too, need the love that HU can bring.

They didn't try to change the parrot, but they knew singing HU would open the way for ECK, the Holy Spirit, to bring divine love into their household.

Humphrey and the Water Bed

A woman had a cat named Humphrey. One evening the woman was lying on her bed reading *Child in the Wilderness*, a book I wrote about my experiences with the Light and Sound of God.

As the woman got to the chapter about my experience with God-Realization on the bridge, Humphrey became very excited. He started running back and forth on the bed. Since it was a water bed, this caused quite a commotion.

Then he grew quiet and just sat on the bed, looking up at the ceiling.

The woman looked up at the ceiling too, but she couldn't see anything. She wondered what had caused Humphrey's excitement. It was because the cat could feel what I was trying to put into the book. I wrote it as well as I could, thinking maybe someday somebody would understand. Maybe the cat did.

Cats have an ability to see into the other planes of God, such as the Astral Plane. They can see the travelers who come and go from the Astral to the Causal, Mental, and higher. If they're friendly people, the cats are just interested; if they're frightening, the cats are frightened.

Animals are Souls too—a particle of God sent here to gain spiritual experience.

Animals are Souls too—a particle of God sent here to gain spiritual experience. For this reason Divine Spirit will reach out and touch them in just the same way that It reaches out and touches you.

In this case Humphrey found out about ECK through his owner reading an Eckankar book.

The White Wolf

*T*hrough daily practice of the Spiritual Exercises of ECK, a woman was moving into a higher state of consciousness. At times, via Soul Travel, she was able to get above her physical body and look back at it.

Her spiritual vision enabled her to see all the organs operating inside her body, with one interesting exception: In place of her heart, she saw a beautiful white wolf.

She asked me, "What does this white wolf mean?"

The wolf is a noble, solitary creature. It responds instinctively to the laws of nature and its own personal nature. In much the same way, Soul, at Its best, responds only to the higher laws of ECK. It will obey them without fail, even as the wolf unfailingly obeys the laws of its own nature.

This woman saw the wolf as being white, and for her white represents purity. This means that her goals in life are of the highest spiritual nature. Her whole life is devoted to ECK, the Holy Spirit.

The wolf image is a variation of the hound of heaven. A wolf is more fearsome than an ordinary hound, however. Therefore, the white wolf at her heart center indicates determination.

This person is very determined to live the life of ECK, and will do so with purity of heart.

In place of her heart, she saw a beautiful white wolf. She asked me, "What does this white wolf mean?"

Love on the Pond

*T*here was a pond behind the former Eckankar Spiritual Center in Minneapolis. In spring a number of ducks would swim around in it.

One of the office staff liked to walk over to the pond on her breaks. The ducks would come up to her and watch her as she quietly sang *HU*, a love song to God.

The ducks seemed to enjoy her song. As she walked, they waddled along as fast as they could to keep up with her. But one day it occurred to her they probably expected her to have food for them.

She made up her mind to bring the ducks popcorn the next time she came. *They'll really like that,* she thought.

At home that evening, she found that her roommate had left half a bag of popcorn in the cupboard. "That's the ECK speaking," she said. "I wanted popcorn for the ducks, and the ECK provided it." She tasted a few pieces, found them a little stale, but decided it was OK for the ducks.

The next day she took the popcorn to work, and at lunchtime she went to the pond to visit the ducks. Some were in the water, and others were walking around on land. She tossed some popcorn at them, but they wouldn't eat it. In fact, they started moving away from her.

She followed after them, urging them to eat, convinced they wanted the popcorn.

She made up her mind to bring the ducks popcorn the next time she came.

The ducks that weren't already in the pond headed for the water, and they all swam away, their tails toward her. She was very disappointed.

She brought the popcorn back into the office and set it on a table. It wasn't too stale for the staff—they ate it all.

A few days later she came back to the pond with toasted whole-grain bread. Seeing two large geese, she figured it must be really hard for them to get food. She tried to give them some of her toast, but they weren't interested. The more she tried, the faster they waddled away from her.

She turned her attention to two ducks standing at the edge of the pond. She threw some toast to them, but they, too, snubbed her generosity. None of them wanted her food. Disappointed again, she headed back to the office.

Suddenly something occurred to her.

She realized what they had wanted from her was the love she gave them through singing HU.

When she had showed up just to sing *HU* to them, the ducks had been much more congenial. She realized what they had wanted from her was the love she gave them through singing *HU*.

Plenty of other people were available to reduce the love to a material substance like bird food, but from her they had come to expect it in its purer form. From this experience, she learned that birds and other animals need love as much as human beings do.

The self-discipline involved in a situation like this is to listen, to know and understand the real needs of the beings around us. The discipline is to be aware. You become aware by chanting your secret word or HU—not constantly but whenever you think of it.

If you can do this, you will find that Divine Spirit will speak to you in many different ways through the world around you.

108

A Spiritual Exercise
to Give and Receive
Divine Love

*S*oul moves through the evolutionary process in a number of different forms, including
those of animals and birds. These are some of
the many different ways in which Soul gains
experience, thereby gaining expression of Its
divine self.

In the process, Soul must learn to receive
love and to give love.

One of the best ways to learn how to give
and receive divine love is to chant *HU* as a daily
spiritual exercise. Simply sit comfortably where
no one will disturb you, close your eyes, and gaze
gently into your Spiritual Eye. This is the point
between your eyebrows, at the center of your
forehead. Then sing *HU* softly on your outgoing
breath.

As you do this, feel within the love that God
has for you and the love that you have for God.
This is why HU is sometimes called a love song
to God.

Few people take the time to simply sit still
and contemplate for twenty minutes to a half
hour each day. Yet when you do this, you open

Continued on next page

your inner senses to the Light and Sound of God—to the pure love of God.

And as you do the spiritual exercises and get more of the Sound and Light of Divine Spirit flowing into you, what are you going to do with it?

You can't spend your life in contemplation of the higher truths without doing anything to bring a little light to your fellow man. One way to start is this: Simply give back some service of love to the world, your friend, your neighbor; and it may be simply by doing a good deed every day that no one ever knows about.

CHAPTER SIX

Animals in the Inner Worlds

Sid the Horse

A husband and wife bought a horse, which they named Sid. Their plan was to train the horse and, when he reached a certain age, resell him.

About a year later, the husband had an unusual dream.

In the dream, he found himself entering a crowded bar. Seeing one unoccupied table, he went over and sat down. A man came over and introduced himself.

"Hi," the man said. "I'm Sid, your horse."

The dreamer thought this was the funniest thing he had ever seen. "My horse in a dream, looking like a man," he said. "This is really wild."

The only thing that bothered him about the dream was that this man had a tooth missing, whereas his horse did not.

The dreamer and his horse got to talking. Sid said, "You know, I love you and your wife. I'd like to stay with you. I've never had owners before who could Soul Travel and meet with me in the dream state so we could talk things over."

This is pretty far out, the dreamer thought.

"Sid," he asked. "I notice you've been limping on one of your hind legs. Is there something wrong?"

"I'm having a problem with that foot," said Sid. "It's just a minor thing, but if you can get a farrier

Sid said, "I've never had owners before who could Soul Travel and meet with me in the dream state so we could talk things over."

113

to trim my hoof, I could walk better." And they continued talking.

When the man awoke and told his wife about the dream, they shared a good laugh over it. She thought the part about the missing tooth was really hilarious.

Later that morning as they walked to the stable, they saw a crowd around Sid's stall. The couple rushed over, afraid that something dreadful had happened to their horse.

There was a little bit of blood on the door of the stall, but Sid seemed to be all right. The husband put a halter on the horse and led him outside.

"If you plan to ride him, just don't put a bit in his mouth," one of the grooms advised him. "Your horse somehow got his mouth caught on the door lock, and his tooth broke off."

Husband and wife looked at each other.

Just as Sid had said in the dream, his hoof needed trimming.

"The missing tooth in your dream," she said. Without another word, they leaned over to check the horse's hind foot. Just as Sid had said in the dream, his hoof needed trimming.

In the dream state, the MAHANTA is the Dream Master. The Dream Master sometimes manipulates the dream state so Soul may communicate with Soul, whatever Its form. Since the man might have totally discounted a dream about a talking horse, the Master changed the image to one the dreamer could accept. This is just one of the ways the Dream Master works.

114

Zeke's Translation

A man had a very old dog, Zeke, who was his special friend. The veterinarian had bad news, though. The fourteen-and-a-half-year-old dog had cancer in his abdomen, but no pain.

He'd probably slip peacefully away, said the vet. But if Zeke developed a breathing problem, it would be time to let him go.

That sad day soon came. The man and his wife took Zeke to the vet and had him put to sleep. Zeke was in the man's arms when he went, literally leaping from that tired old body like a prisoner set free from his cell.

On the drive home, the man's Spiritual Eye opened. He saw Prajapati, the ECK Master who cares for the animals.

Prajapati was standing on a hill near a tree. Behind him came a stream of bright golden sunlight from the sky. But there was also a ball of light, and the man knew instinctively that it was his departed friend, Zeke, in the Soul body.

Zeke's joy was unbounded.

By telepathic voice, Zeke said to the man, "Daddy, I'm free! Thank you for all the love."

Many people love their pets very much and feel a deep sense of loss when they pass over. And they often worry, Is that the end? Does my dear friend simply cease to be?

The man's Spiritual Eye opened. He saw Prajapati, the ECK Master who cares for the animals.

There was also
a ball of light.
It was his
departed
friend,
Zeke, in the
Soul body.

Soul is eternal. Soul lives on in the next world, just as It did in this one.

And, if it is right for that Soul, It can come back to earth in another body, sometimes to the same family It was with before.

Is God's love even sufficient for animals? Yes, it very clearly is—at least it is clear to those who have the eyes to see and the spiritual awareness to recognize this eternal truth.

Good-Morning Bark

A family has a dog. When they travel, they have to put the dog in a kennel. They have cats too, but the cats are self-sufficient. The family can leave them food and water and put them in a room, and they'll be OK.

When the family is home, their young dog has a certain habit. She sleeps all night, but early in the morning, about six o'clock, the dog barks once.

The bark means, "It's been a long night, and I've got to go outside. Now!"

If the family wants to sleep a little bit longer because it's Saturday or Sunday morning, the dog barks one more time—not very loud, but loud enough.

During an Eckankar seminar, the dog was in the kennel, and the man was hundreds of miles away from home. The first morning of the seminar, at six o'clock, the man was sleeping.

Suddenly he heard the bark of his dog, loud and clear. "It's time to get up."

The man opened his eyes, thinking he was home. But he was in a hotel room.

And then he realized that across the miles, the dog had actually said, "Good morning, I'm thinking of you. I hope somebody takes care of me now. I've got to go outside."

What binds people, animals, and all beings to-

Their dog has a habit. Early in the morning, about six o'clock, the dog barks once.

117

Across the miles, the dog had actually said, "Good morning, I'm thinking of you."

gether in this world and in the other worlds? Simply divine love. When the dog barks and the master hears it, even though they're separated by miles, this is a bond of love.

Where the state of consciousness is high in a Soul—whether It has taken the form of a human being, a cat, or a dog—there is this bond of love.

The Two Collies

*O*ne night a sales representative had a dream about two collies. Her recollection of the dream was a bit garbled the next morning, but she dutifully wrote down as much of it as she could remember. Then she went about her life as usual.

She was just sitting down to dinner the next day, when she heard a noise at the kitchen door. There were two collies standing outside.

The woman recognized them immediately. They were the collies in her dream.

If she hadn't had that dream, she might have sent the dogs on their way, thinking that they were simply exploring the neighborhood and looking for a handout.

But because of the dream, she opened the door. Both dogs greeted her like an old friend, and they seemed to be talking to her—trying to tell her something. They nudged her and made moaning sounds. But each refused all treats, food, and water.

The woman got a phone number off one collie's dog tag and left a message for the owner to call her.

Then she grabbed a coat and boots and went outside to be with the collies. They jumped and danced around her, showing complete love and trust.

So she took them for a walk.

Walking up and down the street, she hoped to run into the owner, who might be looking for the

The woman recognized them immediately. They were the collies in her dream.

119

lost pets. She tried some commands on them. "Heel!" she said. They obediently fell into step with her. "Stay!" They stayed. "Come!" Of course, they came running up.

Well-trained dogs, she thought.

Later that day, the owner got her message and called to arrange pickup of his dogs. The collies were delighted. The larger collie began making noises like, "Woo Woo Woo!"

When the owner arrived, he explained that home was three or four miles away. But he was confounded when she told him how they had obeyed her commands. They'd never had training, he said.

The lost collies came to this woman's door because they remembered her love from the dream world where they had already met.

The lost collies came to this woman's door because they remembered her love from the dream world where they had already met.

Sometimes animals will seek us out because they need our help. They can sense if the person they approach is open to Divine Spirit, divine love. Animals are Souls. They may be following an inner nudge, or they may be acting on something they learned in the dream state.

Yes, animals dream too.

A Spiritual Exercise to Be Aware of Your Dreams

*T*o become more aware of the role they play in your daily life, keep a record of your dreams. They will gradually become easier to remember and easier to understand.

This spiritual exercise is called The Golden Cup.

Every evening at bedtime, visualize a golden cup to be filled with your dream experiences. The cup sits by your bed.

When you awake in the morning, in contemplation or in your imagination, drink from the cup. You are drinking in the experiences, a conscious way of saying, I want to remember what I'm doing on the inner planes while my body is asleep.

The golden cup is Soul; it is you. As you put more attention on drinking from the cup, it takes on a life of its own. The more the ECK flows in and out of the cup, the more Soul shines of Its own golden light. You, as Soul, become an ever brighter vehicle for the Holy Spirit.

The experiences you have will lead to greater awareness of your life and its divine meaning.

CHAPTER SEVEN

Animals
and
Healing

Roses, Roses?

"Jennifer" enjoys a strong love bond with her dad's Labrador, "Bella." Jennifer was piqued by the dog's apparent agelessness—all the more remarkable in that her dad didn't walk her or make any other major effort to sustain Bella's fitness level. Yet she seems to be in better health than many other dogs her age. Jennifer wondered about that.

Why her excellent health?

The answer came shortly in a dream. Bella appeared in her usual dog form, which Jennifer could only describe as being in constant equilibrium, with a warm spark of golden light.

That was Bella.

They celebrated their meeting with great joy. Bella explained that this lifetime was to help her grow spiritually. Moreover, her main agreement was to teach Jennifer's father about love. Her message had not yet been fully delivered, so her health would last until her work was done.

They celebrated their meeting with great joy.

She added, "Knowing this, you must not mourn my passing, but celebrate. It means I've been successful in the lesson I've come to teach."

Spiritually, it's roses, roses all the way.

A Spiritual Master
Helps a Veterinarian

*T*his is a story about a vet, a cat, and Prajapati, an ECK Master who takes a special interest in animals.

Our story begins with "Mike." He's a young man. He was riding his bike down on the beach, and there he saw a surfboard. Nobody was around, so he took it home, got on the internet, and went to a site that specializes in help wanted and lost items. He put a notice up—"Found: A surfboard."

A little bit later, he got a call from a veterinarian. He identified his surfboard, and they made arrangements. So Mike took the surfboard over to this veterinarian, whom we'll call "Doctor Ken." Doctor Ken said to Mike, "If your family ever has need of my services, I'll give you a discount."

Not long after this, the family cat became very ill. They remembered the offer from this vet. So they took the cat, Simba, to him. When the doctor came in, he looked at the cat and said, "This cat is very sick." He didn't need to do a whole lot of poking and prodding to see the cat was hurting here, there, and everywhere.

Doctor Ken said, "I'm one of the very few vets who practices energy medicine."

This sort of energy medicine is sometimes called remote treatment, which may be offered by a chiropractor or some other healer. It's very effective, but

Prajapati is an ECK Master who takes a special interest in animals.

it takes a certain kind of patient. I think cats are very open to this sort of thing because it's energy, and cats are very sensitive to energies.

While Simba was being treated, Mike's father told Doctor Ken all about the ECK Master Prajapati.

The next day, Mike's mother, "Ann," came to visit Simba. She saw that the cat was in terrible condition, and she began to cry.

When Doctor Ken came into the room, he started asking all kinds of questions about Prajapati. Then he went on to describe him. He said, "Prajapati came to me in a dream last night. Don't worry. He said everything is going to be OK."

Three days later, Ann went back to the veterinarian. The doctor said, "I've got the blood-test results. But before I call them up on the computer, I want to make sure Prajapati is here." He wanted to go into contemplation, shut his eyes, and be assured that the ECK Master was present. So Ann shut her eyes, and she began to sing *HU*, our love song to God. At the same time, Doctor Ken called on Prajapati.

After a bit, Doctor Ken opened his eyes and said, "He's here. My skin is tingling. I can feel him. Can you feel him?"

Ann said, "Yes, he's here."

Then the doctor turned around, faced the computer, booted it up, and got the results. Finally, he turned back around with a big smile on his face, and he said, "The blood tests are all OK. Everything's normal. You can take Simba home."

The spiritual lesson here is that love is so strong it can reach out through the Divine Spirit, the ECK.

I mentioned an ECK Master. It means a Master who is well attuned to the Holy Spirit. This love had come from the Holy Spirit, through the ECK Master Prajapati, to take care of one of the least of Its own. And this is how life is.

Molly's Diet

*W*hen our dog Molly was about twelve years old, she developed a dry cough that grew steadily worse.

Molly coughed and coughed, night after night. This went on for months. We changed her diet several times, experimenting with different foods. Each new food brought a temporary improvement, but after a few days another allergy which had been lying in the background came forth.

We found a very good veterinarian who worked with a natural means of healing and used medicine only in critical situations. He said Molly's condition had reached a crisis and that it would take an antibiotic to get her past this stage.

But since he felt antibiotics were not good for the animal, he would try to wean her off them as soon as possible. At the same time, he recommended another change in her diet to make her stronger.

We tried the doctor's dietary program. Molly seldom had a cough after that.

But a funny thing happened. At the same time Molly's diet was changing, I began discovering things about my own.

I learned that anything made with flour caused congestion. In the years I lived on the farm, I got too much of it. At some point my body developed an allergy and began to react. So every time I ate any

A funny thing happened. At the same time Molly's diet was changing, I began discovering things about my own.

131

flour products, my body formed congestion to protect itself against this substance that had become like a poison to it. As I got older, my body's resistance and tolerance also diminished, and it began to reject more foods it was able to handle before.

People who watch their pets closely can learn something about healing themselves. There was a parallel between the foods that Molly was sensitive to and the foods that caused us problems. By watching her carefully we learned about ourselves. She got better, and so did we.

If a person has the consciousness to change his diet as his body becomes unable to handle the foods he enjoyed in the past, he is able to work in a better state of health than those who continue with the same diet. The people who won't make changes start to develop a number of ailments, until eventually they can't carry on anymore.

The subject of healing is usually thought to apply to humans, but many of us know it also means taking better care of the pets who give us so much love and companionship.

The Injured Bird

A woman was very depressed. She was going through a financial strain, plus the responsibility of caring for her ninety-year-old mother had fallen on her shoulders.

The elderly woman lived in another section of town. She was very demanding. She would call her daughter several times a day, wanting this or that done right away. She was always complaining about something, and her daughter was at the end of her patience.

In contemplation one day, the daughter asked the MAHANTA, the Inner Master, for help in shaking her depression. Then she drifted off to sleep, only to be jolted awake by the ringing phone.

It was her mother.

"I want you to mail a letter for me as quickly as possible," the older woman said. The daughter started to protest.

"It has to go out today!" her mother insisted.

Looking out the window at the cold, rainy day, the daughter reluctantly agreed to come right over.

She drove to her mother's, got the letter, and headed for the post office. On the way she saw a large white bird standing in the middle of the street. It didn't move out of the way as she approached. She steered her car around it very carefully, not wanting to hurt it.

She headed for the post office. On the way she saw a large white bird standing in the middle of the street.

After she mailed the letter, she came back along the same route. The bird hadn't budged. *There must be something wrong with it,* she thought. *If it stays in the road much longer, it's going to get hit by a car.*

She got out of the car, taking a light coat she had with her. Very gently she placed it around the bird. Then she carried it back to the car and set it on the passenger seat. The bird was quiet the whole time. It seemed to be sick. She decided to take it home and nurse it back to health.

At home, she parked the car and carried the white bird inside. Upstairs she found an old birdcage. She placed the bird inside and gave it some food.

"There's a bird upstairs," she said to her son as he came in the door. "It's so sick it can hardly move."

Her son went upstairs to take a look. A minute later he called down to her. "Mother, I thought you said the bird was sick. It just flew out of the cage."

Running upstairs, she found the bird perched on the curtain rod.

She took the bird to a wooded lot and let it go. Watching it fly away, she realized she felt better.

"Maybe it isn't sick," she said. "But it's such a cold, wet night that I'm going to keep it here until morning, just to make sure it's OK."

The next morning she took the bird to a wooded lot near her home and let it go. Watching it fly away, she realized she felt better than she had in a while. Her depression had eased.

Soon after that her mother fell and broke several bones. Many of the nursing chores fell to the woman and her sister, and with her regular work schedule, the woman barely had a moment to herself.

If her mother had been demanding before, she was impossible now. She expected both her daughters to be with her every day. The ECKist tried her best to please her mother, but it got worse and worse.

One night she fell into bed, exhausted from another endless day. Her mother was running her ragged. *I cannot take one more step,* she thought. *This is more than I can stand.* "MAHANTA," she said, "please take this situation over. I simply cannot go on this way." Then she closed her eyes and promptly fell asleep.

The following day she went to visit her mother. "I had a most restful night," the elderly woman said unexpectedly. "I don't know why, but I'm feeling pretty good."

That day her mother's heavy complaining stopped for good. She still had her little complaints—you don't get out of the habit overnight—but she no longer blew every incident way out of proportion.

The ECK Initiate recognized the help she had been given. She remembered the day her mother had wanted the letter mailed and the errand that led to the white bird. Helping the bird had relieved some of her depression.

Helping the bird had relieved some of her depression.

When she was finally able to admit that she could no longer carry the load by herself, things really changed. When she released the situation to the MAHANTA, her mother had an inner experience that left her in good spirits for the first time in many months.

A short time later the mother was moved to a warm, homey place where she was happy and made new friends. Within a matter of months, the whole situation turned around.

Little Black Kitten

*A*n elderly woman in England had a cat named Scrap that she had to have put to sleep. This was a very great loss for her. Our pets become our very close friends; when they leave, there is a great emptiness in our lives, and we don't know if we'll get another pet.

During one of this woman's empty days, she looked out her window into the garden and saw a little black kitten. Somehow it had jumped over the six-foot fence into the backyard.

"I don't want to start feeding this kitten," the woman said. "It probably belongs to someone else, and it should go home."

But she put food out because the kitten was very hungry.

As time went on, the kitten appeared every morning, waiting for her breakfast.

As time went on, the kitten appeared every morning, waiting for her breakfast. This concerned the woman, but she'd put the food out anyway. Months went by, and one morning she noticed the cat was pregnant.

Soon there were five more kittens.

With five kittens in her care, the woman's freedom changed. She no longer traveled to see friends and family as often. But she also began to notice that the mother cat had some of the characteristics of her old friend Scrap. The woman started to wonder if the young cat was Scrap come back in a new body. So she decided to keep the cat and some of the kittens.

137

She missed her freedom to travel, but she was learning that life is day to day. God had given her someone to love and need her.

We need to be needed in life.

By coming into her life at this time, the little black kitten helped the woman heal her broken heart.

Termites

*F*or many years, a woman had a very bad case of asthma. She had been free of it for three years, but after she traveled one summer, the asthma suddenly came back. It became a fight for breath, just trying to stay alive.

The woman went to a number of doctors. One said, "Cut out certain foods that you have shown an allergy to in the past."

She did that. It didn't work.

Another said, "Here's some medication. Take it. Maybe it will help." It didn't help. The woman was at a loss as to what was causing the return of her condition.

About this time she found that the house she had lived in for eighteen and a half years had termites.

"Termites," she said. "What do I do to get rid of the termites?"

The woman contacted a few of her doctors. "What happens if exterminators come into my house and use poison to kill the termites? What's going to happen to me?" she asked.

The doctors said that, considering her condition, it probably wouldn't be very good for her.

A friend of hers who was a housing inspector happened to stop by about this time. He offered his help to look at the termite problem. As he was checking her home, he looked at her air conditioner. And

"Termites," she said. "What do I do to get rid of the termites?"

"Thank you for sending the termites," she wrote. "Because of them, somebody found out that my home had mildew."

he noticed that the air-exchange unit was loaded with mildew.

Not long after, she sent me a letter of thanks. "Thank you for sending the termites," she wrote. "Because of them, somebody found out that my home had mildew. And the mildew was causing my asthma."

The woman could see that the termites were actually a blessing in disguise. She had the awareness to recognize the steps involved—from termites to mildew to asthma—as Divine Spirit brought her the healing she had been looking for.

Misha's Favorite Toy

A woman had her own business, and all the cares about it weighed upon her. She would go out running every day. One day after her run, she came home worn out and worried. During the run, she'd been thinking: Should she keep her business, or should she accept a job that a nutrition company had offered her which paid very well?

She was sitting there wondering about what to do, tired out from her run, and even more tired from the worries of her business, when Misha, her Siamese cat, nudged her.

Misha had his favorite toy in his mouth. He nudged her as if to say, "Hey, it's time to play. Lighten up. This is my gift of love to you."

The woman began to smile. She felt her heart lighten as she saw the love her cat was giving her. It was a gift from one of God's creatures. Another Soul.

Many animals have an uncanny way of knowing where they should go to get the help they need. Those with a higher consciousness even know where to go to give help to those who need it.

Our pets understand us far better than we think. Wrapped up in our daily concerns, we often don't see what we need to do to stay in harmony with the world around us—but they do.

Misha nudged her as if to say, "Hey, it's time to play. Lighten up. This is my gift of love to you."

Cassius

*A*n ECK Initiate was at her neighborhood park for a walk and got to talking with a woman who was walking her large dog, a boxer. The woman said, "My dog, Cassius, has arthritis. He's only four years old, and it's causing him a lot of pain. I just don't know what to do for him."

The ECKist went home, and for two days she thought about this dog again and again. She wanted to find something to ease his arthritis.

On the third day, she happened to notice her husband was reading an article on a new supplement for arthritis. It was supposed to get rid of the pain of arthritis in animals, at least dogs. She wondered how she could get this information to Cassius's owner. She didn't know where the woman lived.

On the fourth day, in the morning, she opened the door of their home. In the door ran Cassius. His owner was outside, calling to the dog, "Come back here, Cassius."

But Cassius came in the house, lay down at her feet, and looked up at her with great big eyes of love. He just stayed there. He wouldn't listen to his owner.

The woman outside kept saying, "Cassius, come out here," and then she'd say, "I'm so sorry. I'm so sorry." Because they didn't know each other.

"It's all right," the ECKist said. "I've got something for you."

Cassius came in the house, lay down at her feet, and looked up at her with great big eyes of love.

Her husband handed her the article, and she gave it to the woman. "Thank you so much," said the woman. "This is just what I've been looking for."

Sometime later, down at the ocean, the ECK Initiate saw the woman with Cassius and two children. Cassius was playing in the surf just like a young dog. She didn't know if his owner had taken the advice and gotten the supplement, but Cassius seemed to be fine.

And whether or not the experience helped the dog, it helped the ECKist. Every time she thinks of Cassius coming to her home, running in the front door, lying down, and just looking at her with those eyes of love and trust, she says she's been repaid a thousand times. This was a gift that keeps on giving.

Giving God's love to others is the reason we're all here. God's love comes to us directly from God and through others, both people and animals. Part of Soul's lesson is to learn to give this love back to life, to every living thing.

God's love comes to us directly from God and through others, both people and animals.

144

Giving and Receiving Love

A woman in Holland had two cats, a long-haired cat and a shorthaired cat.

Some days she would get busy and start to feel a little empty inside. All of a sudden, she'd hear a meow. It would be the longhaired cat. He'd come over to her and want to give her some love.

On other days, the woman would be overcome with joy about something in her life. She'd hear another meow, and the shorthaired cat would be next to her.

She realized that each of these beings had a different purpose in her life. The longhaired cat came to this world to give love. The shorthaired cat came to receive love.

If she was feeling too much love, the woman gave it to the shorthaired cat. If there wasn't enough in her, the longhaired cat came to give the woman love.

Within the circle of this woman and her two cats, we see divine love working. Divine love works with you and your loved ones, but you need to stop and recognize it.

You ask, "How do I know if I have God's love working for me now?" My answer is the Spiritual Exercises of ECK. Do them. If you have no time for anything else, have time for them.

She realized each of these beings had a different purpose in her life.

Within the circle of this woman and her two cats, we see divine love working.

As you do them, you will get a greater awareness of what you can do to make your life run better.

A Spiritual Exercise to Recognize Your Gifts

Some people never recognize the blessings they receive. Others may look back and realize they've had a gift of healing of some sort. Maybe something has changed at work to make their life better. But it depends upon the individual—how conscious you are.

A spiritual exercise to begin recognizing your gifts is this: Sing *HU* quietly to yourself or out loud. Look at the obstacles in your life that you think are stumbling blocks. Imagine them becoming stepping-stones.

How are they teaching you about yourself? Open yourself and gain greater awareness of this as you sing *HU*.

The teachings of ECK are all about God's love for you. HU is an ancient name for God that is the key to your secret worlds. Once you learn to use this key, you will find a blending of your inner and outer worlds.

You'll find yourself filling with love.

CHAPTER EIGHT

Children and Animals

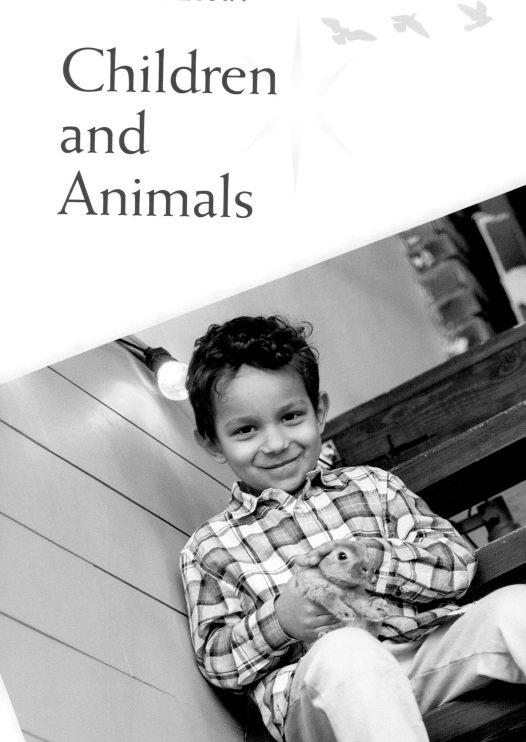

Our Neighbor's Cat

*W*hen my daughter was about seven, we lived in an apartment. One night we heard a loud meowing in the garage beneath us. We finally coaxed a huge orange cat out from under our car, and we called him Sunny. He adopted us just when my daughter was having a hard time at school and was very lonely. This cat became her special friend.

Sunny was huge. Sometimes he would jump up on the window ledge, where he barely had enough room to perch, and scratch on the window to let us know he was there.

Then one day, after my daughter's crisis had passed, Sunny disappeared. She was afraid he may have been hit by a car, and she carried this sorrow for quite a while. I tried to tell her that she had to let go.

Eventually we moved to another home in the same town. One of our new neighbors had a young orange cat named Zack, with whom my daughter formed a very strong bond.

Zack helped her make it through another difficult period of adjustment in her life.

When the couple who owned Zack told us they were moving, my daughter realized there were powers on earth greater than the bond between a cat and a little girl in grade school, and these powers would be pulling them apart. She knew she had to get used to not having Zack around.

Sunny was huge. Sometimes he would jump up on the window ledge, where he barely had enough room to perch.

151

So for two weeks before his family moved, she kept away from him as much as possible. That's when our next-door neighbor brought home Mitty, the little tiger kitten.

When Zack left, Mitty walked in.

The new kitten meowed constantly. He had been taken from his mother, and he hadn't known any other cats. For a while he made quite a racket. My daughter and a neighbor boy tried to figure out ways to make this little cat happy, hugging and holding him so he would feel loved.

By trying to make the cat feel loved, she was able to give her love; and by giving her love, she was able to get love back—not only from the cat but also from the neighbor boy. Up to that point, he and his buddies had picked on her so much that she was almost afraid to go outside. Little boys may like little girls, but not when their buddies are around.

Because of their mutual interest in the little cat, the neighbor boy could now accept her. One day he even invited her to play soccer with him and some of his friends; and because she could kick the ball past them, they began to think of her as one of the guys. He even went so far as to invite her to join his soccer team.

So the mutual interest in Mitty built another bridge for my daughter with a new friend.

There are many spiritual benefits to be had in our contact with animals. This is especially true of children who are lonely and in need of companionship. Animals can often bring them love in a pure, unconditional way.

Four Chickens and a Duck

A young boy had four pet chickens. He was only seven and a very gentle-hearted Soul, so he was always looking for ways to make his chickens happy.

He decided to name them. One was Smart Chicken. Another chicken was First Flyer. And there was Brownie and Speckled Hen. These hens liked this boy; they were very tolerant of his affection. So sometimes he would give them a treat.

The little boy brought out his tricycle, hooked a little wagon to the back, put his little sister in the wagon with one chicken, and gave them a ride.

Speckled Hen rode on the handlebars. That was her special place.

When the boy began school, the chickens missed him. They would go over to the tricycle and look up at the handlebars. They couldn't wait until he got home so he could give them a ride.

The same family also had a duck named Big Wig. It was a white duck with an iridescent purple-and-green head. But at the top of his head, cocked off to one side, was a white feather. Quite a dashing figure, this duck was. And he knew it.

One day Big Wig started to molt, to lose his feathers. They fell all over the yard.

Sparrows and swallows began to take his beautiful feathers to build their nests. The duck got very upset. He ran back and forth across the yard, stretch-

Speckled Hen rode on the handlebars. That was her special place.

ing out his neck and making an awful racket to drive away these thieves. This duck was very much like us people. He was hanging on to something he could no longer use.

The little boy was growing up in this environment. He was learning to care for his pets and other animals, and he was learning to relate to other people in a more spiritually aware way.

Many parents are surprised by how easily their children respond to animals. They forget the good times their children may have spent with animals in previous lives and the intuitive communication—Soul to Soul—that often exists between children and animals.

The Fussy Dog, the Cat, and the Squirrel

A family had a dog that didn't like dog food. He ate cat food, and he ate human food. The children gave the dog carrots and other items they wanted to get rid of. But the dog wouldn't touch dog food.

The family bought many different kinds of dog food. The dog didn't like any of them, and he still went after the cat's dinner. The family finally had to put the cat's dish up on a shelf to keep the dog from eating all the food out of it.

One day the husband was doing his spiritual exercises, and because he did them he had an insight.

He said to his wife, "Feed the dog from the cat's dish. Give it dog food in the cat's dish." And the dog loved it.

> *The husband said to his wife, "Feed the dog from the cat's dish. Give it dog food in the cat's dish."*

Suddenly the dog would eat any of the ninety-nine brands of dog food he wouldn't touch before— if they were served in the cat's dish. And so often this is how we are too.

One day the cat cornered a squirrel in the sandbox out in the yard. The mother and young son ran out to rescue the squirrel, and the dog followed them. The mother grabbed the dog to keep it away from the cat, as the boy grabbed the squirrel. Then the mother yelled, "Let go of the squirrel; it may bite. Grab the cat." So the boy put the squirrel down, and it ran up a tree to safety.

The mother was telling me such things happen in her family every day. She realizes, however, that they are all expressions of divine love.

There is love between the mother and child; that's why she ran outside to help him rescue the squirrel. The dog came out because he loves the cat—and probably he loves mischief too.

In summer, the family decided to give the dog a haircut. When the cat came upstairs that evening, after sleeping all day in the coolness of the basement, there was this strange-looking dog in the house. "Who is this strange dog?" the cat wondered, avoiding him for a day or two. Then the cat realized, "Oh, it's just Sandy," and went back to pestering him.

The dog, cat, squirrel, child, and mother are all different. But something binds them all together. That is the love of God, or the love of ECK.

This divine love is working every day in my life and in your life, and in the lives of your friends and family and neighbors. This love is drawing you together. You need people, and they need you.

The dog came out because he loves the cat—and probably he loves mischief too.

Socks and Spook

A mother took her two daughters, ages eight and ten, to a pet store and returned home with a grey tabby kitten, Socks. All went well for several weeks. Then her son, who had moved to a new apartment where pets were not allowed, brought over his cat, Spook.

Spook took an instant dislike to the kitten. At every opportunity, Spook hissed and swatted at Socks, which soon produced a bloody nose.

Things got worse.

The family even had to nurse the kitten back to health when Spook's claw injured Socks's eye, causing an infection.

In time, though, the two cats became inseparable friends. They soon did everything together.

One day Spook had a litter of kittens. Socks became a second mother to them.

One day Spook had a litter of kittens. Socks became a second mother to them: licking them, keeping vigil with Spook over them, even babysitting when Spook left for a drink, food, or just time off. Day after day, Socks stood in during Spook's break times.

The young girls in the family watched these animals and learned a lot from how the two cats had grown to love each other.

The family later came across an article in the newspaper about whether animals can love. With such a pure example of it in their own home, this family had its own answer. Could there be any doubt?

Only a robot or a person new to reincarnation on earth would say no if asked, Can animals love? Highly evolved people accept it as a fact. They know it because of their better understanding of how God's love actually works—due to their longer enrollment here in the University of Hard Knocks.

Yes, animals can love. There are too many such examples of animal behavior to doubt it. Love goes beyond instinct.

Zsa Zsa and Her Kittens

When I was growing up on the farm, one of my good friends was a black-and-white cat named Zsa Zsa.

Zsa Zsa was a devoted mother. She proved diligent in raising and training her annual litter of kittens. When the kittens were big enough to walk well and mind her mewing commands, Zsa Zsa took them into the cornfield or the oat field to show them how to survive in the wild.

One morning, I heard Zsa Zsa's cry. Her leg was caught in the jaws of a muskrat trap Dad had set in the corncrib to catch rats. I ran out on the front lawn where Dad was holding the trap up by the chain. Zsa Zsa dangled helplessly from the other end. When he released her, she scooted under the granary to hide. Her heartrending cries sounded most of the day.

The other cats tried to console her, but in her pain Zsa Zsa bared her teeth and claws. They retreated and left her alone.

Zsa Zsa was her own doctor. She gnawed off the splintered bone until it was tight against where her fur still grew undamaged. In time, she healed.

Zsa Zsa was a firm, tough lady—missing leg or not.

From then on, she became a common sight around the farm as she displayed her awkward hop. When my little sister brought the food scraps out at noon to feed the cats, Zsa Zsa pushed her way to a prime position at the food tray. Even Lady, the farm dog, gave her plenty of room. Zsa Zsa was a firm, tough lady—missing leg or not.

159

She soon became one of my favorite farm friends. She would hop into the woodshed as I chopped kindling for the kitchen stove. She knew I would soon tire of splitting wood and sit down to rest. The smell of the cookie in my shirt pocket was a further enticement.

Finally, I would set the axe down and wipe the sweat from my forehead. I pulled out the cookie and broke it in two so it would last a little longer. Zsa Zsa sat contentedly in my lap, eating the cookie; then she'd peer expectantly into my face. Would I please get another cookie from the house?

Zsa Zsa sat contentedly in my lap, eating the cookie; then she'd peer expectantly into my face. Would I please get another cookie from the house?

I shook my head. No more cookies. She carefully jumped from my lap, reached back up to my cheek and planted a couple of "thank you" licks on my nose. Then she disappeared out the woodshed door with her peculiar hop.

Uncle Sam beckoned, and I enlisted in the air force rather than face the army's inevitable draft notice. After training, the air force sent me overseas to Japan.

When I returned two years later, I didn't expect Zsa Zsa to remember me. After all, somebody else had fed her while I was gone.

But Zsa Zsa hopped out of the barn to greet me. Her black-and-white fur was still silky and clean, befitting a lady of her position. She was still the queen of the cats. I scooped her up into my arms. Zsa Zsa meowed softly, lovingly, saying how glad she was to see me again.

Suddenly, she struggled to get out of my arms. I let her down to the ground. She seemed intent on some important errand and quickly disappeared into the tall grass.

Then Zsa Zsa reappeared with a soft meow. There was a freshly caught mouse in her mouth. Gently, she laid it at my feet.

I was her prodigal son, one of her many kittens come home. She showed no prejudice in matters of the heart. Zsa Zsa loved me like one of her own. She meowed again, looking expectantly into my eyes as if to say: "Go ahead, eat it! I got it just for you! This is your homecoming present!"

For once, I declined a gift of love.

For a young man growing up, Zsa Zsa was a very special friend. She taught me a great deal about life and the qualities needed to survive the tests and trials of this physical world.

I was her prodigal son, one of her many kittens come home.

Paul Twitchell and Ringo

*P*aul Twitchell was the modern-day founder of Eckankar and author of many ECK books. When he was a child, Paul had a dog called Ringo. He took Ringo to school when he was in first grade. Paul and Ringo were very close friends.

Ringo was a black dog, with white legs and a splash of white across his face. He had one black eye. He was a very patient and good dog, and Paul said that later the teacher began to give Ringo a report card too—always on behavior, because that's the only thing the teacher could grade the dog on.

Ringo always got an *A*. Paul didn't say what he got.

The teacher began to write little notes on the dog's report card like, "Never speaks unless spoken to, and doesn't smell like a dog." Paul said that was true. Ringo never smelled like a dog.

Ringo loved children. He'd lie at the back of the room, thumping his tail on the floor, picking up what he could about ABCs and one plus one. Ringo went to school until the sixth grade when Paul graduated. The junior high school wouldn't allow dogs, so that was the end of Ringo's education.

But by then Ringo was getting old. He had put in enough years of his life getting an education, and he was probably wondering what he was going to do with this education anyway. So from that time on, he stayed at home and enjoyed sleeping.

The teacher began to give Ringo a report card too—always on behavior, because that's the only thing the teacher could grade the dog on.

Paul Twitchell brought out the teachings of Eckankar in their modern form in 1965. He used to say how important it was for children to have a pet of some kind—if at all possible. It was very important for him to have a pet when he was young.

A pet gives complete attention and devotion to the owner. Some people need this, especially children.

A pet teaches children how to love, or at least it doesn't shut off the loving which is normal and natural for children. It gives them an outlet. It's a very important foundation for the future.

A Simple Exercise to Appreciate Your Animal Friends

*A*t different stages in our life we find it very, very helpful that Divine Spirit has sent us a good animal friend—a dog or a cat or a parakeet, even a goldfish. Something to show the divine love that is so necessary for all beings.

In this exercise, you practice keeping an open heart throughout everyday life. It's very tough; I have to work at it all the time too. No one technique will work for everyone, but there are ways to keep your attention on having an open heart.

So here's the spiritual exercise: If you have a pet, love your pet. Love it a lot. As the love comes, let it pour through you. And show your love by how you treat your pet every single day.

The habit of love is catching; it builds, gains momentum, and becomes easier. But like a plant that needs daily watering and loving care, the habit of love takes constant attention.

Love won't come through unless the heart is open.

To work with an open heart is to love or care for something or someone more than you do for yourself. This is the first step to the divine love that we are looking for.

CHAPTER NINE

In the Master's Garden

First Come the Sparrows

One summer I got a bird feeder. I thought it would be nice to have. With the feeder came a little bag of seed, maybe two good cupfuls.

I put the post in the ground, then set the bird feeder on top. It reminded me of an old street lamp, except there was birdseed in it instead of a wick. I hoped the birds would be able to figure that out.

All morning I watched through the window to see what would happen. No birds.

Even after I sat down at my desk to work, I called to my wife, who was in another part of the house: "Any birds yet?"

"No birds," she said.

How do the birds find the feeder? I wondered. *Is it enough to just put out the birdseed?*

All of a sudden my wife called to me, "Look, there's a sparrow!" I was so happy that I left my work and ran to take a look. It would have been nice to find a pretty songbird, but a house sparrow was OK too.

By the end of the day there was a little group of five to ten birds at the feeder. By the next morning, twenty or thirty birds. And over the next couple of weeks, as many as seventy or eighty birds a day were visiting.

First the sparrows came, then blackbirds. Next the red-winged blackbirds and cardinals. After that,

How do the birds find the feeder? *I wondered.* Is it enough to just put out the birdseed?

169

crows. One night my wife looked outside and saw a gray squirrel. Soon there were two, then four.

The gray squirrels ate off the ground where the sparrows had so generously thrown the feed. But then they climbed up to the feeder and dug the feed out by the pawful. Within a matter of minutes, the bird feeder was empty.

I bought a squirrel baffle, a round plate with a hole in the center, to put on the pole just underneath the bird feeder. Our squirrels couldn't get around it, though I did take a picture of one trying.

When winter came, all the birds left except the sparrows. I knew I would have to feed them during the winter, because they had come to depend on that feeding place.

The cold weather also brought the little red squirrels. They moved like greased lightning. Now we had two kinds: the gray squirrels, which are considered pests, and the red squirrels, which are about half the size of the gray ones.

One evening my wife looked out the window and spotted two rabbits. Periodic observation revealed that the rabbits showed up about ten-thirty at night and four o'clock in the morning.

Then one day, two ducks walked up to the bird feeder. I noticed one of them was trembling from hunger, so I filled a dish with seed and put it out on the ground. Then I put a second dish out for the squirrels.

I had started out with a small bag of feed, then went to a five-pound bag. Then I was buying twelve pounds at a time, then twenty. The last two times I ended up buying fifty-pound bags of seed. Once you start to feed the birds, you require more and more seed; but somehow, there's always enough money and time to keep it up.

When winter came, all the birds left except the sparrows. I knew I would have to feed them because they had come to depend on that.

You also find a great deal of love while seeing to the well-being of those Souls who look to you for at least some of their sustenance.

And so I learn from them. I learn that since I feed them, I have a responsibility to feed them some more. But as we watch them through the window, they give us so much pleasure that we think of them as God's gift to us.

You find a great deal of love while seeing to the well-being of those Souls who look to you for some of their sustenance.

171

Donald and Daisy

*E*arly in spring, we had two mallards, a drake and a duck, fly in to feed in our yard. They soon became regular visitors. Being in charge of the naming committee, I called them Donald and Daisy.

Donald and Daisy commuted. They would land on the lawn next door, then waddle very slowly over to our lawn and eat from the dish I had set there for the animals.

Daisy ate while Donald kept an eye out for predators. I don't know when he got to eat. As soon as she was finished, she'd waddle back to the landing area and take off. Donald would follow, though sometimes he'd glance back at the dish as if to say, "Do we have to go now?" But he always went with her.

Eventually Daisy didn't show up anymore. Maybe she was busy caring for her young. Donald kept coming to the feeder by himself, though, but now he got to eat.

Whenever the blackbirds or blue jays came by, he would stand back and let them at the dish first.

Donald liked peace, and he stayed peaceful even when the rabbit came to the seed dish while he was still eating from it. Actually, it looked kind of ridiculous to see them eating out of the dish at the same time, the duck on one side, the rabbit on the other. Donald used the water dish too, because he needed both the seed and the water.

Donald stayed peaceful even when the rabbit came to the seed dish while he was still eating from it.

173

One day we received a notice that our neighborhood was preparing for a summer spraying program to prevent the growth of weeds. It gave the date this was to take place.

"I don't want them to spray the bird-feeding area," I told my wife. "The birds and squirrels and rabbits have come to trust the seed that I put out there. If I don't do something quickly, these people are going to spray poison all over their food."

There wasn't much time left. Rummaging around, I found some twine and a bunch of little stakes.

I hammered the stakes into the ground and strung up the twine, fashioning a six-inch-high fence all around the feeding area. Then I made up signs that said, "Bird-Feeding Area—Please Spray Around," and stuck them on the fence stakes.

I happened to be at home when the people arrived to put the herbicides on the lawn. Rushing outside to greet them, I asked them not to go within the feeding area. They were very accommodating. The fence made it easy for them to see where not to spray.

That afternoon, Donald flew in like a screaming jet, then took five minutes to waddle over to the feeding area.

The single strand of twine that formed the fence stood about as high as his beak. Donald stood and looked at it, but he wouldn't go inside. *He really is some kind of duck,* I thought, as I watched from the window. *He respects the spiritual space of others.*

"Jump, you silly duck," I urged him. "Get over that little fence."

He just stood there.

"Don't make a fool of yourself," I said, "the neighbors are watching."

174

But Donald wouldn't jump or fly over the fence. He just stood outside of it and gazed longingly at the seed and water dishes I'd left on the ground for him.

Donald had grace.

As you observe the birds and animals, occasionally you find a very special creature, like Donald. He had grace. Animals like Donald are very special indeed.

They have something to teach everybody.

The Rabbit and the Marigolds

*O*ne year, I began to plant flowers in the front yard. It made me very proud when the neighbors came by and said, "What pretty flowers you have." As long as we are here on earth, I feel we should leave it just a little bit better than we found it.

That first year I spent too much time each day grooming the geraniums I had planted. You don't have to, but they look better if you do.

So the next year I got smart and planted marigolds. You cannot destroy a marigold. You put them in the ground, and that's pretty much it.

Every evening just before the sun went down, a rabbit would come into our yard to wait for feeding time. But one evening I went outside to find him eating the marigolds I had planted.

"What are you doing?" I scolded him. He looked at me in surprise and shock.

"What are you doing?" I scolded him. He looked at me in surprise and shock. He couldn't figure out why this nice man who had provided him with these flowers was suddenly behaving this way.

Puzzled, he scampered off to hide.

"I feel really bad about the rabbit," I told my wife, "but the flowers have rights too."

For a while the rabbit stayed away. Then one day, I saw the marigolds weren't blooming. They had nice green leaves but no flowers. I fertilized them, but they still didn't bloom.

"Maybe the rabbit's eating the flowers again," I complained to my wife.

"He wouldn't eat the flowers," she said. She always defends the rabbit.

"Just wait till I catch him."

So I kept looking out the window, and suddenly there he was in the backyard, eating the buds off the marigolds. I couldn't believe my eyes. He even went up to a big, full, yellow flower and opened his mouth.

He went up to a big, yellow flower and opened his mouth. "He wouldn't dare," I said.

"He wouldn't dare," I said, then watched as he took a big chomp out of it, leaving only half a flower.

I called to my wife, "The rabbit did it again!"

"No! He didn't!" she said.

"If you hurry, you'll see where the yellow went." But by the time she got to the window, the rest of the flower had disappeared into his mouth.

After that, I decided to come to an agreement with nature. If I want to plant flowers, that's my business; if the rabbit wants to eat them, that's his business. We get along fine now.

I smile at him, he looks back at me, and that's how we pass our time.

We both love flowers.

Backyard Community

*A*fter a few seasons, I got rid of our bird feeders on poles. They were just too much trouble in the winter. Yet I continued to put dishes on the ground for our backyard varieties of birds, raccoons, squirrels, rabbits, and chipmunks coming to feed.

Then one day a beautiful six-point buck and a doe showed up at the feeding dishes. I heard a loud noise outside our window and looked out to see the buck bumping the doe out of the way. He wanted all the food for himself.

The deer is a symbol of gentleness, but that huge buck was not living up to his character.

The rabbit, whom we called Stretch, simply sat at the dish opposite the buck, about four or five feet away. I was so proud of Stretch. He didn't back off at all. The buck hadn't learned anything about gentleness, but the rabbit—often a symbol of fear—was sure learning something about bravery.

The animals in our backyard make up a spiritual community. They are all learning lessons about when to come to the feed dish, and they all have their scheduled times. The rabbits and the squirrels are about equal. If the rabbit comes and finds the squirrels are already there, he waits. If the rabbit is there first, the squirrels get a little pushy and boisterous, but they wait until the rabbit decides to leave the dish.

Then there's the chipmunk.

He's a little bitty guy, but he has plenty of nerve. He'll come out of the woods, so short he can hardly see over the grass. You can actually see his trail into the brush because his belly is so close to the ground.

The chipmunk will see the squirrels gathered around one of the dishes, come up behind them, and zip right through their group.

Every time, he scares the living daylights out of them. They all go scurrying up the trees. Then the chipmunk takes one more swing through the turtle-doves, who go flying up in the air.

Pretty soon he has the dish all to himself.

He doesn't have a lot of grace, but he does get the dish.

I've noticed, too, that the squirrels outrank the blue jays. If four or five squirrels have the dish, the blue jays have to wait. But they're smart—and loud. They'll start screeching and shrieking the way birds do, with their little screams of "Danger! Danger!" When the squirrels run off into the trees, the blue jays come down and take over the dish.

The animals and birds that come and go in our backyard community are part of our family. Sometimes they fight with each other over the food—sparrows with other sparrows, cardinals with other cardinals—yet they are a family. In their own way they get along.

A Spiritual Exercise
to Learn from the Birds

*S*ome years ago I worked with a man whose hobby was bird-watching. At the time I didn't really understand what he saw in it. But I have since come to appreciate his love for birds.

They have so much to teach.

Birds are working off their karma too. You often see them fighting with each other. In the bird pecking order, sparrows are at the bottom. Blackbirds are a cut above the sparrows, blue jays are above the blackbirds. One day I saw a little yellow bird drive off a blackbird and a crow. It chased them all around the yard. Like spiritual seekers, some birds come as eagles, not as doves. And like the yellow bird, we're small but feisty, if we need to be.

So, as a spiritual exercise, feed the birds. Your job is simply to bring the food and to learn from them. Watch how they show us how to act and how not to act.

They often show us the love and wisdom of God.

CHAPTER TEN

Communicating with Animals

Do Not Disturb

A doctor in one of the African countries had just left the hospital where he worked. As he started his walk around the building, which would take him past a fruit tree, one of the nurses came up to him.

"Doctor, don't go that way," she said. "There is a cluster of bees in that tree."

Following her pointing finger, he saw what looked like a huge ball attached to the little tree. "The bees came about two days ago," the nurse said. "Everyone at the hospital has been avoiding that path. We are afraid they might sting."

There were so many bees that the stings could have been fatal.

As they discussed ways to get rid of the bees, the doctor told her, "When I was a boy, I used to set the grass near the bees on fire and try to smoke them out." Boys have ingenious ways to take care of problems. I know, because I did—and I paid my karmic debt for them.

"There are many things we could do," the doctor said, "but they all involve using force. That is not necessary. The bees will go when they are ready, and they will leave as quickly as they came. Let's not disturb them now."

He went back into the hospital and returned to work. Five minutes later the nurse came over to him.

"There are many things we could do," the doctor said, "but they all involve using force. That is not necessary."

"I should have come to you two days ago, Doctor," she said. "You won't believe this, but every bee is gone."

The doctor was surprised too. Even though such experiences often occur in the life of an ECKist, they don't become commonplace. We're still learning. Things don't always work out the same way. Under different conditions, the bees might not have left.

About two months later, just as the doctor arrived at the hospital early in the morning, the same nurse ran up to him to report another problem.

"Doctor, an ox has gotten into the hospital compound. What should we do?" She had gained an extra amount of respect for him since the bee incident. She figured he knew something about handling creatures that others did not.

The doctor thought back to his boyhood days, when he would chase away an ox by throwing stones at it. The ox might run away or it might come after you. Either way, you got it to leave the place where it wasn't wanted.

So the doctor went to the fenced area where the ox was chewing grass, and picked up some stones. But as he watched the animal, he thought about how he would feel if he were at his breakfast table and somebody came along and threw stones at him.

He put the stones back down on the ground.

"What are we going to do about this ox, Doctor?" the nurse asked.

The doctor opened the gate leading out of the hospital compound. He went over and stood near the ox. "Finish your breakfast," he said to the animal. "When you are done, please leave by this gate."

With those words, the ox gave a sudden jump, as if it had just received a shock. The doctor stepped back and watched.

The ox went back to eating the grass and continued for about five more minutes. When it was finished, it turned toward the open gate and leisurely made its way out of the compound.

The doctor may not have realized it, but as he spoke to the ox, he was sending it love. If we can learn to do all things with love, we have come a long way on our journey home.

Soul often communicates on the inner planes through telepathy—not the kind we sometimes find here on earth, but a finer kind. It is also possible to communicate through the transference of images. When animals communicate with people, it is usually through this latter method, the transference of images.

There are times, however, when the communication takes place via a greater power. And the ECK, the Holy Spirit, is able to work through us at a time when our heart is open to God's love.

Sunshine and Sparkle

A couple had two cockatiels, beautiful birds about eight inches tall. The couple had taught them how to say a few phrases, such as "Kiss, kiss" or "I love you." Sometimes they would say, "Sweet baby."

One day the male bird, Sunshine, began putting words together in his own way, and they made sense.

He would run after Sparkle, the female bird, come up behind her, and say, "I love you, sweet baby." Then he'd make a kissing noise. Sparkle put up with it. But sometimes she got tired of his talk; she turned her back and walked away from him. Poor Sunshine, all full of this love, would then go up to a mirror, look at his reflection, and say, "Hello, sweet baby. I love you."

When Sparkle saw him doing this to the mirror, she thought it was a waste of endearments. So she'd run back to him. Then he could say his sweet nothings to her.

Sunshine noticed that the man of the house would jump up when the phone rang. Pretty soon, Sunshine learned how to imitate the sound of a telephone ringing.

The man would hear the phone ring. He would run to answer the phone, and nobody would be there. Then he'd look around the room, and in his birdcage, Sunshine was ringing. Which of course

The male bird, Sunshine, began putting words together, and they made sense.

189

meant, "Come over. Pick me up. I want love." So the man would go over and give Sunshine some attention.

When it got near bedtime, Sunshine would start making the ringing sound. He didn't want to go to bed. But finally it was time to put the cloth over the cage, to put the birds in a dark place so they could get some sleep.

Then morning came, and Sunshine was there to greet the person who pulled the cloth off the cage. If the woman of the house took the cloth off, Sunshine was very sweet. "I love you," he'd say.

But when the man took the cloth off the cage, Sunshine would say, "Hello?" That's because he was the one who picked up the phone when Sunshine made the ringing sound.

Two cats also lived in the house. One, an adult cat, was a very definite threat to the birds. When that cat got near the cage, the birds squawked in warning. Even Sunshine wouldn't talk. But when the young cat came near, things were different. Maybe Sunshine thought there was time to convince the young cat about being a good person—befriending birds, for instance, instead of having them for dinner.

When the young cat came near, Sunshine would say, "Are you my sweet baby?" trying to convert him.

So Sunshine would say, "Are you my sweet baby? Are you my sweet baby?" The cat, of course, had no idea what this all meant, that Sunshine was trying to convert him.

Sometimes, when the day had been rough, the man of the house would come home from work and listen to the news of all the unrest and political corruption around the world. But in the safe little haven of their home—with the dog, the cats, and the cockatiels—he could settle down and rest for the evening.

The love in this family was the real shelter. When they shared love, they could get themselves together and gain the strength to face tomorrow.

The Cat Who
Got the Cream

One day a cat had an eye infection. So his owner took him to the vet. They came home with herbal eyedrops to use. The woman tried to put the drops in the cat's eye, but he would fight and fight.

The woman called the vet. "I think you'd better give me another kind of eye treatment; the cat does not like these drops." She brought her cat in again, and the vet said, "Yeah, he needs something else."

He gave the woman a cortisone eye cream. She tried to put it in the cat's eyes, and he fought worse than ever.

So the woman put the cortisone cream away. When she came back later to get the tube and again try to put this eye treatment in the cat's eye, the tube was gone. She looked all over, and she finally found it hidden in a corner of the room, with tooth marks all through it. The cat had punctured the entire tube.

She found it in a corner of the room, with tooth marks all through it. The cat had punctured the entire tube.

She called the vet again. He said, "I think we'd better check this over one more time." When she brought the cat in, the vet said, "Yes, I've got to change the prescription."

Then he said, "This is the first time I've had one of my patients tell me, in no uncertain terms, to change the prescription."

193

The vet said, "This is the first time I've had one of my patients tell me, in no uncertain terms, to change the prescription."

The woman had the awareness to hear what her animal friend was telling her. Perhaps it was not so difficult in this instance, since the cat spoke loud and clear.

The best way to listen to our animal companions is to see them as Soul. This means recognizing their eternal spiritual nature and knowing that God loves them just as much as God loves you.

Molly and the Air Conditioner

Our little dog, Molly, had such fragile health in her later years that my wife prepared her food very carefully and prepackaged the portions. Everything was homemade. She gave her vitamins and herbs and a lot of love.

Molly was very sensitive to temperature changes. This was a challenge in Minneapolis because we have huge weather swings. It can be very hot, then cold, then rainy, then dry, then hot, and so on.

Early one spring I awoke to a hot, muggy morning that promised to get worse. I turned on the air conditioner and waited for the house to cool off. A few minutes later my wife came in and said that Molly had started to catch a cold the day before because of the air conditioning.

Molly was the strangest dog I'd ever seen, maybe because she was a house pet and I was more used to the kind of dogs we had when I lived on the farm. Whenever it got too hot outside, they would lie down in the shade with their tongues hanging out. The hotter it got, the less they moved. Molly, for some reason, did it backward: the hotter it got, the more she jumped up and ran around.

Her comfort range required that we keep the temperature within a three-degree span; one degree higher was too hot, one degree lower was too cold.

Molly was a house pet, and I was more used to the kind of dogs we had on the farm.

195

My wife spent most of her day either working at her desk or checking the temperature in whatever room Molly happened to be in.

So I turned off the air conditioner and went back to my desk, and my wife went to take a shower. All of a sudden I heard her say from the bathroom, "That's strange."

"What's strange?" I asked.

"The bathroom fan turned on by itself," she said. It had never done that before. "I wonder what that means," she added.

It occurred to me that the ECK was trying to tell us to turn on the central fan to keep the air moving. It would blow air through the vent near Molly's bed, but it would not chill her.

And so we did.

Sometimes animals will let us know when they have a message for us, but we need to give them our attention if we are to hear what they are saying. In this case the ECK intervened to show us what would help.

Guests for Breakfast

A couple in Finland had a nice homestead with over three thousand currant bushes. They also had a colony of ants. Every day the ants would march all the way from their nest to the currant bushes.

The couple didn't mind this. The ants kept the vermin away.

But there was one small problem.

During the summer months, the couple liked to eat breakfast outside at a picnic table. But the path the ants took to get to the currant bushes went right under the table. And since the table was fixed in position, they couldn't move it to another part of the garden.

One day the wife decided to talk with the ants. "Could you please move your nest?" she asked. "We love you, and we don't want to step on you by accident as we're having breakfast."

A couple of days later, she and her husband were seated at the table having breakfast. She looked down and saw all the ants carrying eggs and other items. They were moving their nest several yards to the north.

The woman's request had been heard by the group entity of the ants. Families of animals have a group thought form or guiding entity, similar to the group entity that runs the Borg in *Star Trek*. In much the same way there's a group entity, not just for ants but for all animal communities.

One day the wife decided to talk with the ants. "Could you please move your nest?" she asked.

197

The wife had addressed the group entity of the ant colony, and she had spoken with love. And the ants took her words in the spirit of love.

Saving Isabella

*O*ne day a woman was taking a shower. She opened the bathroom door, and Misha, her Siamese cat, did something he'd never done before. He jumped to the top of the bathroom door and perched up there, like a hawk.

She wondered, *Why is Misha acting so strangely?*

The woman knew that animals often work in images, so she made herself still inside and tried to put herself in Misha's little booties. She got a picture of Misha's daughter Isabella stuck on a high fence separating their yard from a neighbor's. If Isabella toppled over to the other side, it would have been very hard for the woman to get the kitten out of there.

She quickly got dressed and went outside.

Sure enough, there was Isabella, stuck on the fence, wobbling back and forth, trying to keep her balance.

The woman picked the kitten up off the fence, and Misha and Isabella were both very grateful for her help. They knew it was a gift of love.

When we give our animal friends our attention and listen with our heart, we can often hear what they are trying to tell us.

She got a picture of Misha's daughter Isabella stuck on a high fence.

Birds in the Fig Tree

A man used to put cheesecloth on the family's fig tree to protect the fruit from the birds. This worked very well. But one day, as his wife was working at the kitchen sink, a hummingbird flew up to the window.

The tiny bird flew back and forth, from the kitchen window to the cheesecloth-covered tree, then back to the window.

The woman said, "Something's wrong."

She went out to the tree and found that a young hummingbird had been caught underneath one of the folds of the cheesecloth and couldn't get out.

When the woman lifted the cloth, the young bird flew out and joined the mother hummingbird. The two birds simply fluttered there for a minute in front of the woman, hovering in midair as if to say, "Thank you for this gift of love."

Then they flew off, very grateful for her act of kindness.

The woman also had a gift of love from the Holy Spirit. It was knowing in her heart that she had done something to help another of God's creatures.

The tiny bird flew back and forth, from the kitchen window to the tree.
The woman said, "Something's wrong."

A Spiritual Exercise
for Gratitude

*W*hen you need to open your heart to love, try this spiritual exercise. Not only will it help open your heart, but it will help to keep it open.

The technique involves attitude, and it is one that must be lived. In a word, it's called *gratitude*.

It is a joy to be around people who live by this principle. They know what they've got is precious, even if it does not amount to much materially. Most of all, they have the gift of life. And because they appreciate this gift and feel grateful for it every day, they also have the gift of love.

Animals, too, have an awareness of this principle and often express it in ways we can understand.

So throughout the day, contemplate on all the blessings in your life.

This practice will help you begin to recognize your own individuality as Soul and the incredible love that God has for you. And as you see and accept the love of God, you will learn to love yourself more. Then you can love others more, be they human or animal.

CHAPTER ELEVEN

Animals and Reincarnation

What Can We Learn from Our Pets?

*P*eople who are new to Eckankar are sometimes surprised when they hear us refer to cats and dogs as Soul. In ECK, we do regard our pets as Soul. Why? Because they are.

They're a creation of God—just as surely as we are. When a cat translates, or dies, something leaves just as surely as when a human being dies. When a baby takes its first breath of life, something comes in. This happens just as surely as in a kitten.

Human vanity likes to say, "God made us and put a Soul in us," as if you can possess Soul. But in Eckankar, we say, "We are Soul." We are Soul, and through successive lifetimes, we take on a body for whatever experience we need that time. Sometimes it's a male body, sometimes a female body.

We don't get into transmigration, where we go back down the spiritual evolutionary scale to the animal or the mineral state. That's lifetimes and lifetimes past. But it also doesn't mean that this evolutionary scale goes straight up—or that it goes from plant to animal to human, where people can look down at their dog or cat and say, "Well, you are Soul, but I am a greater Soul because I am human. You still mess on the floor."

Some animals—I would say a great number of animals—probably have a higher state of consciousness than their owners.

We don't get into transmigration, where we go back down the spiritual evolutionary scale.

207

People go to work. They become angry, they cheat if they can, and they indulge themselves in things that hurt both their physical body and other people who are dear to them. Then they come home, and the cat is always there, the dog is always there.

Treat your pets right, and they'll always love. They don't look at you with the eyes of judgment, saying, "You've got alcohol on your breath again." Cats and dogs won't do that to you. They'll love you even if you've just had Limburger cheese. They'll probably want some. "Just pet me, and let me sit in your lap," they say. "Be kind and good to me."

Cats and dogs are very nonjudgmental. In this way, they're often superior to human beings.

We see somebody who is bumping the electric fence, a little bit out of the rhythm of life according to our idea of what the rhythm of life is, and we say, "This person is doing such and such. That person's head is sticking up higher than everybody else in this social group." That is the social consciousness speaking. We get very self-righteous about our opinions. We think we are always walking around in shiny clothes and other people are always walking around in dirty rags. We are special.

Well, dogs and cats don't mind. Especially dogs. To dogs, their owners are always walking around in shiny clothes, because they're always giving out food.

208

Dream Kitten

A woman had a female cat for a pet. They had lived together for eleven years, and there was a very strong bond of love between them. Eventually the cat died, and the woman missed her very much.

About a year after her cat had died, the woman had a series of very clear dreams. In one dream, someone told her, "Your cat is going to reincarnate on Monday, July 31."

When the woman woke up, she said to herself, *That dream was very nice. But I live in an apartment in a big city now. I don't know how my cat is going to find me.*

Then she had a second dream. In this dream someone handed her two tiny kittens.

Both kittens were striped; one was lighter, the other darker. The Inner Master told her, "The darker of the striped kittens is yours."

That week one of her friends called. "Two of my cats had litters at the same time," she said. "Would you like a kitten?"

When the woman went to look at one of the litters, she immediately saw the striped kittens from her dream. "This is my cat," said the woman, picking up the darker of the striped kittens.

"It's a male," said her friend.

The woman paused. "A male?" she said. "My cat was a very feminine female. I can't imagine her com-

In one dream, someone told her, "Your cat is going to reincarnate on Monday, July 31."

ing back as a male cat." Suddenly she was unsure of her dream.

Her friend said, "If you want a female, there's a lovely gray-and-white kitten in the other litter. This kitten loves everybody." But the kitten didn't love this woman.

"All right," sighed the woman, putting down the clawing animal. "I think I'd better stick with the first striped kitten."

On her way out she asked her friend, "By the way, what was the mother cat's name?" "Z," said the cat owner. Z is another name for the Inner Master, Wah Z.

As she drove home, the woman said inwardly, "Maybe this really is my cat, even though it's a male."

Later, before her daily contemplation, she picked up *The Shariyat-Ki-Sugmad*, the Eckankar bible. She opened the book at random and read, "Soul will alternate between male and female bodies, each time learning some lessons while gathering karma and working off karma."

The woman had the answer she needed.

Animals are often examples to people of how the spiritual laws work.

The Crying Cat

A woman kept a kennel for cats. People who were going on vacation brought their cats, and she took care of them. She loved cats and built very big cages for them. Her business cards had mottoes like "We love cats" or "Love is everything."

The kennel gave the cats a lot of space and a lot of freedom. The cats were happy; they were happy to go home when their owners came back, or they would have been happy to stay. Life was pretty good for the cats.

Except for one cat named Busy. Busy was a good cat. But whenever the kennel owner would walk out of the room, Busy would begin to cry.

Cats can really make a racket if they decide to cry, like some people crying to God. No one could stand it when Busy cried and cried and cried.

By about the fifth day, the woman's roommates were going crazy with the noise. They'd go out to eat just to have some peace and quiet. Everyone was losing their sanity, and they didn't have much love left.

The kennel owner began to be very angry at Busy. The crying cat was destroying the love and harmony that had been in the kennel.

Finally the woman turned the situation over to the MAHANTA, the Inner Master in ECK, the inner side of myself. "MAHANTA, I can't do anything," she

Whenever the kennel owner would walk out of the room, Busy would begin to cry.

211

said. "If you or any of the other ECK Masters can help, please do something. The cat's driving me out of my mind."

That night, the kennel owner had a dream. In her dream she saw Prajapati, the ECK Master who takes a special interest in animals. Prajapati came up to Busy, picked up the cat, and began petting it.

As he petted the cat, a golden heart appeared on Busy's chest. Busy loved the attention and quieted down.

Soon other ECK Masters appeared in the woman's dream. Busy was happily running back and forth from one ECK Master to another, enjoying all the attention and petting.

Rebazar Tarzs, an ECK Master who used to serve in Tibet, picked Busy up. "Busy, let's go for a little walk," he said. And he took the cat to a dark cave that was nearby.

When they came to the entrance, the ECK Master said, "Busy, this is a cave, and we're going to go inside. It's very important for you to see and understand what this cave means to you." They walked inside and saw a deep pit.

Rebazar explained that the cat had walked by such a pit on the physical plane in a previous life, fallen into it, and cried to get out. No one could hear its cries deep in the cave. So the cat had perished.

This terror had stayed with the cat into this present life.

It was the source of Busy's fear of being left alone. As Rebazar explained it to the cat, the golden heart on Busy's chest began to shine, casting light around them.

"How would you like to explore the cave?" Rebazar asked the cat. In other words, explore the source of your fear.

Busy became like an ordinary cat, very inquisitive. They walked through the cave, and the Light of God came through the golden heart and lit up the pitfalls, holes, and other dangers.

The next morning, when the woman went to see Busy in the kennel, the cat was quiet. She had seen in her dream what happened to the cat on the inner planes. And from that time on, Busy never had the crying problem again.

Truth reveals itself through the Light and Sound of God. Whether it comes to an animal, to you, or to someone else, it fills your heart with love. And when your heart is full of love, what room is there for fear?

The woman had seen in her dream what happened to the cat on the inner planes.

Tiger Lily

A thirteen-year-old girl moved to a new town with her family, and she was lonesome. One day, she was with her mother, sitting in front of a store on some bags of fertilizer. The father was inside the store, paying for supplies. As the mother and daughter were sitting there, all of a sudden they saw something moving behind the bags of fertilizer.

It was a black-and-white kitten. It seemed lost, so the thirteen-year-old girl put it inside her shirt and carried it home.

When they got home, the girl showed the cat to Dad. He wasn't real happy, but he said, "All right, you can keep it."

This cat was a companion for the girl for almost twenty years. They were together until she turned thirty-two.

This cat was a companion for the girl for almost twenty years.

The woman had found that the longer they were together, the more she loved the cat. Her love for the cat grew deeper and deeper. And about that time, she read one of the stories in the *Eckankar Journal,* an annual magazine with stories by members of Eckankar. The story told of a cat owner whose cat had reincarnated to be back with her.

The woman knew it was getting near to the end of the cat's life. So she began telling her cat, "Tiger Lily, if you ever want to come back, please come back. Because I love you."

Finally it was time for Tiger Lily to go. She had

spent many good years of happiness, love, and service on this earth.

For two and a half years after the cat was gone, the woman wondered, *If Tiger Lily ever comes back, how will I recognize her?* She tried to think of some symbols, something that might work, something out of the ECK teachings.

The woman wondered, If Tiger Lily ever comes back, how will I recognize her?

How would she be able to recognize her dear friend Tiger Lily?

About this time she got married to a wonderful man. And this man had a wonderful dog. Unfortunately, the dog liked to chase cats. Now the woman worried, *If Tiger Lily comes back, how will things work out with the dog?*

One night the woman had a dream. In the dream she suddenly knew that Tiger Lily was back. When she woke up, she said, "I know Tiger Lily's back now. I'd better talk to the dog and see what the dog feels about this. How would the dog like a cat here?"

So she began talking with the dog. "How would you like a cat?" she asked. The dog wagged his tail. The woman took it as a good sign.

The woman began to notice people giving away kittens. Each time she saw this, she wondered, *How am I going to know? Is that the kitten? Is that Tiger Lily?* Finally she said to the MAHANTA, "I don't think I'll be able to figure this out with my head. I'm just going to have to trust my heart."

One day, she was over at her husband's parents' place, and they had just had dinner. The couple was ready to leave, when a young kitten came running down the street.

Cats are very nonchalant about things like reincarnation. "There's my owner," the cat probably said as she came running up to the woman. "I've been waiting for you." This woman looked at the kitten.

It didn't look like Tiger Lily, but she picked it up.

The kitten immediately licked her on the nose and began purring. The woman's head was spinning. She had waited two and a half years. She had wondered, *How will I know? I don't want to get the wrong cat. I want to get Tiger Lily.* And here was this kitten, so glad to see her, licking her nose and purring.

Her mother-in-law said, "I know where that cat belongs. It lives down the street. We'll go ask the family if you can have it."

"No, no," the woman stammered. "I don't know."

But the mother-in-law said, "Come on. We'll go over there." So she dragged this woman over to the neighbors. "Go on and ask them," she said.

The woman still couldn't talk. She was stammering, unable to get any words out.

Her mother-in-law said, "Could she have this kitten?"

The neighbors said, "Sure. And if it doesn't work out, just bring the kitten back."

There were problems at first. The dog did like to chase the cat, so they had to work with the dog. And the kitten hadn't been completely house trained, so there were messes on the rugs. But each time the woman looked into the cat's eyes, she could see it was Tiger Lily. There was no question.

Her old friend had come back.

It didn't look like Tiger Lily, but she picked it up.
The kitten immediately licked her on the nose and began purring.

Lulu and Misha

Siamese cats can be very finicky and self-centered. But not Misha.

When his owner was sleeping in the morning, Misha lay very, very still. Most cats are different: as soon as they are awake and hungry, they start moving around, maybe licking your face. "Breakfast time. Let's get up and go outside." But not Misha.

Misha also had a habit of jumping into his owner's arms, just wanting to be loved. And after he got hugged and loved, then it was time for breakfast. But loving always came first.

After a while, his owner began to notice there was a very close connection between the love that Misha gave and the behavior of a toy poodle she used to have named Lulu. Misha was acting a whole lot like Lulu.

There was a very close connection between the love that Misha gave and the behavior of a toy poodle she used to have named Lulu.

Lulu used to love to jump into her arms too. And Lulu used to have a blanket that she chewed holes in. The woman had stored it in the closet.

She wondered, *Has Lulu come back to me as Misha?*

One day, when the woman came home from work, she saw that Misha had climbed into the closet and pulled out this big, heavy blanket that the dog used to play with.

A Siamese cat is not quite as big as a toy poodle. Misha had pulled and dragged this thing out into the center of the room and then sat there. So when the woman came home, wondering, *Could Misha be Lulu come back?* the first thing she saw was the cat sitting on the blanket, speaking in the only language it knows, in the language of symbols.

Misha was sitting on Lulu's old, chewed-up blanket, sitting there with a smile on his face, saying, "Get it?"

Soul is eternal. It never dies. The body dies, but Soul never dies. Since we cannot learn all that this world has to teach us in just one lifetime, we come back in another body and continue with our spiritual education.

What could be simpler? Furthermore, the principle applies not just to humans but to animals too. How can it be otherwise, since they, too, are Soul?

All of us have lived before.

Misha was sitting on Lulu's old, chewed-up blanket with a smile on his face, saying, "Get it?"

A Spiritual Exercise to Learn about Past Lives

*S*ometimes there's a strong bond between people and their pets, or a bond with certain other people. And we wonder, *Why such a strong bond?*

Often the answer lies in a past life.

If we had the ability through a dream experience, Soul Travel, or the intuitive powers of Soul to understand this connection between that other Soul and ourselves, it would clear up so many things. It would let us treat other people with more love and kindness, because we'd have an insight into our relationship with them.

The inner worlds are as real as this outer physical world. There's a connection between the two. Sometimes if things aren't working right out here, instead of going through years of karma and trouble, you can get things back on track if you know how to go to your inner worlds.

As a spiritual exercise, before going to sleep sing *HU*, the love song to God, a few times. Then ask the MAHANTA to take you to the inner worlds for an experience where you gain the insight either to change conditions or to improve yourself. Keep a pen and notepad at your bedside to

Continued on next page

write down any insights when you awaken.

Sometimes this is all that's required to help things work better in the physical world.

CHAPTER TWELVE

All Souls Are Going Home to God

Baby Robin

*I*n a tree behind our house lived a family of robins—mother, father, and three babies. One afternoon I was working in the yard, when I heard the sound of a very small bird in distress. So I went over to investigate.

A robin had fallen out of the nest; it stood at the base of the tree. The parents were very distressed, yet their instincts said to feed only the ones in the nest.

I watched for a while to see what would happen. I figured maybe the parents would carry food to the robin that had fallen out of the tree. But the parents never brought it food; it looked as if they were just going to let it starve.

The baby robin began to peep. It was afraid. It looked up at the nest: it knew home was right there on the end of the branch with leaves on it. But it couldn't get back up; it was too young to know how to fly.

Every so often it would try to tell itself, "I'm a big bird; I'm not afraid of anything." Then it would sing the song of a full-grown robin. The peep-peep of the frightened baby bird and the very confident song of the grown robin alternated as the little bird was torn back and forth.

OK, I thought, *I've got to do something.*

I went into the garage and looked around for something to use to pick up the baby robin. A little garden trowel and a stick looked right.

To pick up the baby robin, a little garden trowel and a stick looked right.

When I approached the bird, it gave me a sour look. "You touch me, and I'll . . . ," it seemed to say.

You'll what, little bird? I inquired silently. I pushed it up onto the trowel with the stick and lifted it toward the nest.

About this time one of the adult robins came back. It began screeching at me, "Don't touch my baby, please don't hurt my baby," making this big commotion. I was trying to get the little bird into the crowded nest, and it didn't want to go. Its brother and sister spread their feathers to show there wasn't a lot of room.

"This is your only chance," I explained. "If you want to grow up, get in."

I nudged the bird with the stick. "This is your only chance," I explained. "If you want to grow up, get in."

The bird was looking at me with as much anger as it could muster. It was probably thinking, *A steel trowel and an ordinary stick. My word!*

Finally I got the little robin into the nest. The others made room for it, and the parent sat on a branch nearby, hopping around, scolding, very nervous.

The next day when I went out to check on the bird, all three babies were still in the nest. Two of them looked so innocent, with their little beaks open toward the sky, waiting for Mom and Dad to fly in with another worm. The third baby had his mouth shut and his eyes open, giving me the same sour look as the day before.

"You're not the first one," I told him. "I've helped others and gotten just as much thanks."

The little birds in the nest are like Soul before It finds truth. It's safe and secure in Its small world. Somebody takes care of Its needs, and life is perfect.

Then gradually life becomes less and less perfect

as these little creatures grow bigger and it gets crowded in the nest. And there are stirrings within the robins. They say, "Our destiny must be something greater than this nest. We want to go into the world and see if there's something else out there besides worms."

The little birds in the nest are like Soul before It finds truth.

The natural order of life is spiritual unfoldment and growth. Whether anyone likes it, believes in it, or accepts it or not, life says you're going to grow spiritually.

Someday you're going to outgrow your state of consciousness. Someday you'll become a Coworker with God.

This is your spiritual destiny.

Mitty the Kitten

*T*here was a young cat in our neighborhood named Mittens. We called him Mitty for short. He was a friendly little thing, but from what I could tell, he had never been a cat before.

Mitty was an orphan, so he didn't have a mother to set an example for him. Nor had he ever studied himself in the mirror to see that he was a cat: he had two pointed, fuzzy ears, a button nose, and tiger-striped fur.

Because he didn't know he was a cat, Mitty thought he was a human being. The little boy who took care of him was short, and he was a good ball-player, so Mitty probably thought he'd grow up to be one too. He was relating to what was nearest to him.

Because he didn't know he was a cat, Mitty thought he was a human being.

One day Mitty must have decided that being a boy wasn't really his destiny. He spotted a big black tomcat walking around, claiming his territory, and Mitty began to study him. The little tiger-striped kitten followed the big black cat everywhere he could, watching how he walked and trying to figure out what the tomcat was thinking about.

But whenever Mitty got too close, the tomcat would turn around and attack him as a warning.

The first time it happened, the kitten ran away and hid in the bushes. But as soon as the big black cat moved away, Mitty began to stalk him again.

I watched him one day. "You fool, Mitty," I said. "Don't you know what's going to happen? That cat is going to attack you again."

But Mitty was learning how to be a cat, and you can't learn something like this at a distance. By getting close, he found out that cats have sharp claws, they growl, and they make a ferocious spitting sound.

Pretty soon Mitty learned to leave the black cat alone. Next he found a white cat, bigger yet. This cat was friendly to humans, but he didn't like kittens following him around. Maybe because the new cat wasn't black, Mitty didn't associate this species with danger, so he began to follow him around.

Mitty was learning some valuable lessons, and like it or not, he was growing up to be a cat.

Again, he got his ears boxed and his little head pounded in the dirt. Mitty was learning some valuable lessons, and like it or not, he was growing up to be a cat.

One afternoon, while walking along the back fence, he saw a beautiful Siamese cat. Mitty just couldn't help himself—he had to get a closer look. She attacked him too. He took off along the top of the fence, tore through the hanging branches, and lost some of his fur in passing.

But Mitty was patient; he was learning. He crept back along the fence and hid behind the branches, still watching and studying. I was watching Mitty while petting the Siamese cat, Angel. She's a very jealous cat: If I was petting her, that meant I belonged to her, and she certainly wasn't about to share the attention with Mitty.

Mitty continued to grow up quickly. He soon began to feel his strength and claim bigger parts of the territory. He no longer limited himself to the little plot of grass in front of his house; more often than not, he roamed other people's backyards and crept along their fences.

It was just a matter of time before he was strong enough to prove himself to the rest of the cats. He probably even took back some of the fur he lost.

As Souls who want God-Realization, this is how we are too. Because we've never been God-Realized before, at first we don't know how to go about it.

One way is to observe someone you feel has a golden light flowing from within. Start by observing someone who lives the kind of life that you want to live.

If you practice the Spiritual Exercises of ECK for a few minutes every day, you will lay the foundation for God-Realization. Like Mitty, you may not quite know what to expect, but the subtle hand of the Holy Spirit will begin to work in your life as never before.

This is how we are too. Because we've never been God-Realized before, at first we don't know how to go about it.

231

Gizmo and the Orange Cat

*G*izmo had been a certain woman's cat for thirteen years. Throughout a period when the woman was ill, Gizmo had shown her how to have patience: "Hey, slow down. Relax. Don't worry about things."

The woman was learning about unconditional love. Love is worth more than many treasure chests full of gold. If you have all the gold in the world and not love, you have nothing.

Then, one summer, Gizmo suddenly became very ill himself. It was clear to the woman that he had to be put to sleep, but she agonized. Can I do it? Should I do it? Should I not? Back and forth, all the questions.

As she was asking these questions, the word *mercy* came into her mind, and she realized that God is love and mercy. The Ocean of Love and Mercy is God's home, the place where God dwells.

She knew then it was to be done.

Two days after the passing of her cat, the woman and a friend were sitting on the porch, talking about Gizmo and remembering. Along came this young orange cat. He ran along two neighbors' lawns, right up onto the porch. He ignored the friend and went right into the woman's lap. He just sat there.

She had never seen him before, but he made

Two days after the passing of her cat, this young orange cat ran onto the porch, right into the woman's lap.

233

himself right at home. He wanted to play. He wanted to make her laugh. He ran out on the grass, did acrobatics, chased a grasshopper, and just had a great time.

It was almost as if Gizmo was there, telling the woman through the cat, Look at this young cat body. I got rid of my old one, and I'm going to get a new, healthy body.

The next day this orange cat visited again; he came right into the house. He searched the counter, nosed around, and found Gizmo's toy mouse. He played with that for a while. Then the woman lay down, as she had often done with Gizmo, and this orange cat plumped down on her chest and put his head underneath her chin. He went to sleep for an hour.

She was thinking, *Wow, just like Gizmo.* Gizmo used to do the very same thing.

The third day the cat came back to make friends with her husband and look around outside a bit. After this third visit, the woman was very curious.

She asked some of the neighborhood kids, "Is there a cat around here—a young orange cat?"

They said, "Oh, yeah, two blocks over."

But the cat never came back, and she never saw him again.

The orange cat's visits were a sign to the woman that Gizmo was sending love and comfort. Gizmo was saying, "Hey, Mom, I'm OK. I'm going to come back in a young, healthy body, and there will be many more good times, if you want."

That's how love works. It knows no bounds.

The Shariyat-Ki-Sugmad, Book One, says that the Law of Love is "the great principle of life. Its simplicity is amazing for it is summed up in the statement:

Soul exists because God loves It. In other words, all life exists because God so wills it. This is the very foundation of life, the whole of the philosophy of Eckankar. There is nothing more, and nothing less."

These are the blessings of love.

Our destiny lies in the Ocean of Love and Mercy. All Souls are going home to God. They may take the long route, the short route, or any number of detours, but it doesn't matter. One way or another, by the path of their own choosing, all Souls are going home to God.

One way or another, by the path of their own choosing, all Souls are going home to God.

An Ant's Point of View

*W*hen my daughter was in grade school, she liked little things—snails and roly-polies and fuzzy caterpillars. And she liked ants. Sometimes I would tease her about it, kid her on to a new understanding.

"Do ants have feelings?" I asked one day. "They are so small. It makes me wonder if they have feelings."

And then I said, "They're like children. They are so small. I wonder if they have feelings." I said these things to help her grow up.

"Oh, Dad!" she said, aware that I was teasing her.

"Well, suppose the dad ant," I continued, "who was known to have a great consciousness, explained the way of man to the child ant. He would explain to the child ant that man was a huge thing that thundered past with big, earthshaking steps. The wise father ant would explain to the child ant that, in reality, ants know nothing more than left, right, backward, forward. Suppose he said, 'Someday, we will evolve in consciousness to where we can create great vehicles that will fly us wherever we want to go, all over the world. We will also create something that will record pictures of the past, present, and future.'"

I paused, studying my daughter. I could see that she was thinking about the ant story I had been telling her.

237

Then I continued, "The little child ant looked at the father ant. She knew that her father was supposed to be wise, but what he was saying sounded crazy. 'Gosh, Dad,' the child ant blurted out, 'what are you talking about?'

"It is the same with us," I told my daughter. "Most people see only the world directly about them. They haven't seen what we can evolve to be. We don't ever become God, but we can get the God Consciousness. We can become one with Divine Spirit, and in so doing, we get the God Consciousness. Then we become a Coworker with God. The ant story explains that there are levels of awareness far beyond us. If I were to talk about them, you wouldn't understand."

As we unfold, our understanding of God changes. How can it be otherwise? Many scientists today reject the existence of God. But the concept they are rejecting is a very primitive one. They have not yet unfolded to the point where their understanding of God is compatible with the findings of science. They forget that this Physical Plane is but one of many and that the Ocean of Love and Mercy lies far beyond anything their minds can conceive.

This is why I emphasize love so much.

Thinking and reasoning will only take you so far. They are needed for survival in this physical world. But love—pure, unconditional love—will take you all the way.

I told my daughter, "Most people see only the world directly about them. They haven't seen what we can evolve to be."

238

The Dogged Cat

A woman and her husband had ten cats. When the family had moved to a beautiful new home about a mile and a half from their old one, everybody was happy except this one cat.

Cats are lazy by nature, and they will usually not exert themselves, especially down in Florida where it's hot. But this cat had an opinion, an opinion that was stronger even than its tendency toward laziness.

So every morning it would get up when the family went off to work, and it would walk one and a half miles through the heat to their old home. And there it would sit, because that was its home, and that's where it was going to stay.

The first night when the woman came home, one of her old neighbors called and said, "Hey, your cat's here."

So she got in her car, drove over, and got the cat.

The next day, the woman got another call. It was her old neighbor again. The cat had come back.

After working all day, the last thing she needed was to jump in the car and chauffeur a cat around. But she did it.

When the bond of love is strong, you will do anything for your child, whether the child has fur, feathers, or skin. You'll just do anything for it, because this is divine love showing itself down here on earth.

One of her old neighbors called and said, "Hey, your cat's here." So she got in her car, drove over, and got the cat.

And it's one of the finest and most noble things: human love expressing divine love.

This went on for eight months.

For eight months this cat would get up every morning and walk a mile and a half, and then the woman would go over at night and get it.

First, she would drive up. And then she would call the cat. The cat would come running, she would open the car door, and the cat would jump in. The cat started to look forward to the end of the day when Mom was coming. The cat was at the curbside waiting for her, just like a child waiting for the school bus.

The neighbors would come out most nights to watch.

It takes a long-suffering human mom or dad to put up with this sort of thing, but that's what love is about. It is long-suffering. It is long-suffering and patient. Patient almost to the ends of the earth.

The new home was like a new state of consciousness, a new heaven. But the cat was attached to the old one. It did not want to move. It did not want to change. In fact, it behaved like it was on the end of a big rubber band.

Just like the cat, Soul is sometimes unable to detach Itself from an old state of consciousness. So, like the mom, the Master tries to move the individual to a new place. But there's resistance. And the person keeps going back to the old state.

People are always thinking that the old way is better. Why? Because change is such a difficult thing to come to grips with. Nobody likes to change, because changing from one state to another is a spiritual process. Nobody likes to do this, because it means having to do something unfamiliar. And everybody likes to do the familiar thing.

> *The cat was at the curbside waiting for her, just like a child waiting for the school bus.*

> *Just like the cat, Soul is sometimes unable to detach Itself from an old state of consciousness.*

240

But at some point Soul, or the individual, like the cat, says, "OK. I can see the advantages to the new home. I'm finally used to it. And it's just not worth the trouble going back to that old state of consciousness. There are a lot of advantages in my new home. I like this place." And above all, we don't have this wear and tear on the body as we did before.

To accept the higher values is to accept more of God's love. Many people aren't ready to do that, because the more love you get, the more you must give. And that's a responsibility that requires growing into.

The Watchful Heron

One day, a new addition to the regular birds and animals in our backyard family was a young least bittern, a member of the heron family. A large bird, standing about a foot tall, it normally lives in marshes, swamps, and even city wetlands.

Its diet is usually frogs, tadpoles, and minnows. But in our yard, it tracked a bounty of insects, the result of a cool, wet year.

The least bittern is a graceful bird. Most comfortable in the open yard, it patiently stalks moths, grasshoppers, and crickets all day long. It fixes its whole attention upon the intended prey, inches closer in slow and graceful movements, then with lightning speed snaps up the target in its long beak. Immediately after, it seeks a new insect.

My wife, watching from our window, said, "This bird is a good example of how much the spiritual student needs to focus upon the goal of God-Realization."

This little heron has a single goal at a time, moving toward it with grace and patience.

Very true, indeed. This little heron has a single goal at a time, moving toward it with grace and patience. After catching an insect, the bird immediately seeks another target, for its very well-being depends upon an ability to focus upon a single goal at a time, reach it, then quickly move on to find another.

What is its purpose? Even though it spends much of its day in pursuit of food, it, like you, has a very important place in the scheme of creation.

Its hunting and eating are merely activities that fulfill a strong instinct for survival. However, like you and all other creatures, it exists for the purpose of getting experience, the reason for life here.

We can see and understand things today that would have made no sense to us ten or twenty lifetimes ago. Growth is a gradual process. A child in grade school can't wander into a class three or four grades ahead of him and expect to understand what the teacher is saying. But when his time comes, he will.

Soul unfolds over many lifetimes. And with each step, our awareness expands more and more.

A Spiritual Exercise
to Come Closer to God

*H*ow badly do you want God-Realization? Since you have never had God-Realization, what must you do to get it?

If you want God in your life, then focus on God. Invite the MAHANTA to help you do this. If you fill your heart with love, you will find you are drawn toward your goal like a moth to the flame.

Start by singing *HU* on a daily basis. As you sing *HU*, the love song to God, you are making it easier for yourself to become aware of your inner reality. This is a first step.

Then, if you want to remember your dreams or have an interesting experience in your inner worlds, before you go to sleep simply ask the Inner Master, who is also the Dream Master, to assist you. If you do, he'll be with you, whether you are aware of him or not.

You can say, "Dear Wah Z (my spiritual name), I would love to learn more about myself as Soul and come closer to God. I would love to explore the inner worlds while my body is asleep. Please give me some assistance, if this is OK."

When a person takes up the path of Eckankar and works with the MAHANTA, the lessons come

Continued on next page

faster. They also come in a way that is streamlined to his spiritual needs. By connecting with the Light and Sound of God through a daily practice of the Spiritual Exercises of ECK, the student in Eckankar gets to learn lessons on many levels at once, not just here on earth but in the dream state as well.

All Souls are going home to God, and all religions based on the Law of Love will assist in this process.

What makes Eckankar special is that it cuts out all the detours and helps Soul travel home by the shortest route possible.

Questions
and
Answers

*A*s spiritual leader of Eckankar, I get thousands of letters from seekers of truth around the world. All want direct and useful answers about how to travel the road to God. I reply personally to many of these letters.

Here are several questions of interest I've been asked about animals and their spirituality. Read on for clues that may help you too.

Who Chooses Whom?

Do pets choose people?

When my wife and I are driving or walking down the street, we'll see an owner come along with a dog or two or more. And there is such a resemblance. You can look at them and say, "Do you think they're of the same family?" Man and beast, or beast and the high form of life called dog. Human nature being what it is. I ask my wife sometimes, "I wonder how that dog picked its owner, because they look so much alike. How do they do it?"

A woman had lost her cat; the cat had run away. So the woman would go down to the animal shelter every day to see if her cat had been brought in. One day she saw this beautiful golden-white cat waving at her. Cats are not stupid. And so, of course, she took that cat home. What else can you do?

> *"I wonder how that dog picked its owner, because they look so much alike. How do they do it?"*

Do Animals Create Karma?

My daughter saw an animal shelter in our city in which dogs suffer from very bad care. They live in extremely small boxes made out of concrete blocks. Some of these dogs have gone crazy. Since we both love animals, my daughter wants to know why these dogs have to suffer so badly and live under such cruel conditions.

When people suffer and live in bad circumstances, I can explain it with the Law of Karma and rebirth. But how can those animals have broken the spiritual laws? I didn't know how to answer her question. Could you please explain if animals create karma too, and if so, how?

Suffering is not always a direct result of breaking a spiritual law. Even though everyone gets *adi karma*, the primal karma that starts us off in our first lifetime, there is far more to the spiritual journey. A Soul may intentionally choose a hard life to learn more about love, wisdom, and charity. Pain, like joy, is simply a tool in the toolbox of karma and rebirth.

To grow spiritually, we move beyond a strict acceptance of karma and thus take the high road to God.

You can, as spiritual beings, try to make your city shelter a more livable place. Talk to the owner or manager. If that goes nowhere, visit or call your city hall. Each time, ask the MAHANTA what steps to take, then go one step at a time until the conditions in the city's animal shelter are more humane.

An ECKist need not be a helpless cog in the machinery of life. You answer to a higher law: divine love. Use your spiritual powers of creation for the good of all.

Do Animals Have Souls?

Do animals have Souls?

We are most aware of Soul in the human form, and so people, in their limited state of awareness and understanding of spiritual knowledge, generally say, "We have a soul; people have a soul." As I've said repeatedly, we *are* Soul, and as Soul we *have* a body—an important distinction.

Animals, birds, and people are pretty much alike, because we're all Soul.

This consciousness, or this element of Soul, reaches to all levels of creation. Most people have a long way to go in their understanding of God's creation. To think—as people in the Middle Ages did—that human beings are God's highest creation is one of these self-loving behaviors of the human race. It's like saying, I am aware at my level and I have created a God in my image; therefore this God I have created loves me more than anyone or anything else.

This element of Soul reaches to all levels of creation.

This, to me, is not understanding divine love. God's love extends equally to all creatures—human, animal, vegetable, mineral. If a person understands this, then that person has the beginning of wisdom.

I know I'm stretching the boundaries of consciousness for some, but I think it's an important point to make. Spiritual awareness goes far beyond the human mind. The human mind tries to put a tag on awareness and say, "This qualifies as worthy of God's love because it's called a human being. Other things do not qualify for God's love because we call them animals."

And yet as we look through history sometimes we have to ask, Are humans more like animals or are animals more like humans?

Animals and Dreams

Do animals dream?

Like us, all animals dream. Some remember, many don't. Specially gifted ones, like spiritually advanced people, do Soul Travel. In time, scientific research will be able to expand its knowledge of what happens when people and animals sleep.

You can begin exploring your interests in these fields of knowledge through dreams or Soul Travel. Eventually, science will catch up to the knowledge of those who already can explore the spiritual states of living beings—human or animal—by Soul Travel.

Animals and Healing

Can pets help us to heal?

Cats and dogs each give love in their own way. Pets bring healing from loneliness and are companions at times when our own kind won't have us. Sometimes pets are closer to us than our family, because they don't judge us—unless, of course, dinner's late. They need a *real* reason.

Cats and dogs have their jealousies, but they don't gossip. Generally all they want is to love and be loved. People who have a difficult time accepting love from others sometimes find it easier to accept love from a pet. This companionship offers a healing which makes life bearable for them.

When Soul takes up residence in bodies other than the human form, such as that of a dog or a cat, It's just at a different level of consciousness. But Soul in any form is from God, the SUGMAD; and God is love.

Soul in any form is from God, the SUGMAD; and God is love.

Animals and the Holy Spirit

Does the Holy Spirit communicate to us through nature?

The Holy Spirit speaks in ways so subtle, so humble, that most people overlook It.

Actually it isn't that the ways of the ECK are too humble to see. It's that people are too proud to listen. We are too proud to listen, for example, when the earth says, "Please, don't dirty me," or when the animals say, "Please let us live too." And so we defile the earth and harm the animals with the vanity that only man, of all the creatures on this planet, can claim.

The Holy Spirit works and speaks to us through Its creatures and through nature. If we have the spiritual understanding and vision to see, It tells us and shows us in countless ways how the laws of God really work.

If we have the spiritual understanding and vision to see, It tells us and shows us in countless ways.

About the Author

Sri Harold Klemp is a living spiritual teacher, guide, and Master. He teaches about every dimension of the spiritual life. Love shines through his stories and insights about the true nature of Soul. He is the featured columnist for the *Animals Are Souls* blog.

Growing up in a Wisconsin farming community with cows, barnyard cats, dogs, and a variety of country creatures gave him practical experience with the often hidden world of animals. Later in life, from the window near his writing desk, he observed animals in nature. He met neighborhood pets on his walks. Animals often became his inspiration and models for presenting spiritual principles.

After attending divinity school in his youth, Harold Klemp continued his search for truth. *Autobiography of a Modern Prophet* chronicles his journey from orthodox religion to being known today as a pioneer of "everyday spirituality." As the Living ECK Master, he is the current leader in a long line of spiritual Adepts stretching throughout history, touching every culture of the world.

Each year, he speaks to thousands at Eckankar seminars. Using a storytelling style, he helps people take a closer look at what can help them achieve their highest goals in life. His sense of humor delights audiences as he speaks about a breadth of topics, including how animal behavior mirrors human foibles.

He is an award-winning author of more than a hundred books, many of which have been translated into more than twenty languages. For over fours decades, he has continued to produce inspiring spiritual-study discourses, books, articles, stories, and videos. His mission is to help people find greater spiritual freedom, wisdom, and love in their lives.

Next Steps in Spiritual Exploration

- **Browse our website: Eckankar.org.**
  View or subscribe to the *Animals Are Souls* blog; watch videos; get free books, answers to FAQs, and more info.
- **Attend an Eckankar event** in your area.
  Visit "Find a Location" (under "Engage") on our website.
- **Enroll** in an ECK Advanced Spiritual Living course.
- **Read additional books** about the ECK teachings.
- **See "Contact Eckankar," page 260.**

Advanced Spiritual Living

Go higher, further, deeper with your spiritual experiences!

Eckankar offers enrollment in Advanced Spiritual Living courses for Self-Discovery and God-Discovery. This dynamic program of inner and outer study unlocks the divine love and wisdom within you. It offers step-by-step advances in enlightenment through initiation.

From the first day of membership, you can have direct experience with the God Current and begin to meet life's challenges on the highest possible ground.

You will enjoy monthly discourses from the spiritual leader of Eckankar, Sri Harold Klemp, creative spiritual practices for daily life, and the quarterly *Mystic World* publication. Optional classes with like-hearted Souls are available in many areas.

Here's a sampling of titles from the first course:

- In Soul You Are Free
- Reincarnation—Why You Came to Earth Again
- The Master Principle
- The God Worlds—Where No One Has Gone Before?

Books

You may find these books by Harold Klemp to be of special interest. They are available at bookstores, from online booksellers, or directly from Eckankar.

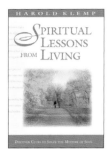

The Mahanta Transcripts Series

The Mahanta Transcripts, books 1–18, are from Harold Klemp's talks at Eckankar seminars. He has taught thousands how to have a natural, direct relationship with the Holy Spirit. The stories and wonderful insights contained in these talks will lead you to deeper spiritual understanding.

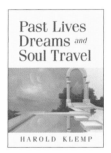

Past Lives, Dreams, and Soul Travel

These stories and exercises help you find your true purpose, discover greater love than you've ever known, and learn that spiritual freedom is within reach.

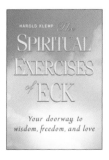

The Spiritual Exercises of ECK

This book is a staircase with 131 steps leading to the doorway to spiritual freedom, self-mastery, wisdom, and love. A comprehensive volume of spiritual exercises for every need.

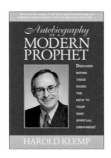

Autobiography of a Modern Prophet

This riveting story of Harold Klemp's climb up the Mountain of God will help you discover the keys to your own spiritual greatness.

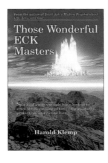

Those Wonderful ECK Masters

Would you like to have *personal* experience with spiritual masters that people all over the world—since the beginning of time—have looked to for guidance, protection, and divine love? This book includes real-life stories and spiritual exercises to meet eleven ECK Masters.

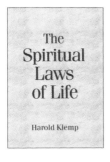

The Spiritual Laws of Life

Learn how to keep in tune with your true spiritual nature. Spiritual laws reveal the behind-the-scenes forces at work in your daily life.

Contact Eckankar

For more information about ECK, to order ECK books, or to enroll in Advanced Spiritual Living courses, you may

- visit ECKBooks.org;

- enroll online at AdvancedSpiritualLiving.org (click "Start Your ECK Adventure");

- call Eckankar (952) 380-2222;

- write to
  ECKANKAR, Dept. BK 55
  PO Box 2000
  Chanhassen, MN 55317-2000 USA.

Glossary

Words set in SMALL CAPS are defined elsewhere in this glossary.

Arahata   An experienced and qualified teacher of ECKANKAR classes.

chela   A spiritual student of ECKANKAR.

ECK   The Life Force, Holy Spirit, or Audible Life Current which sustains all life.

Eckankar *EHK-ahn-kahr*   The Path of Spiritual Freedom. Also known as the Ancient Science of SOUL TRAVEL. A truly spiritual way of life for the individual in modern times. The teachings provide a framework for anyone to explore their own spiritual experiences. Established by PAUL TWITCHELL, the modern-day founder, in 1965. The word means Coworker with God.

ECK Masters   Spiritual Masters who can assist and protect people in their spiritual studies and travels. The ECK Masters are from a long line of God-Realized SOULS who know the responsibility that goes with spiritual freedom.

God-Realization   The state of God Consciousness. Complete and conscious awareness of God. To love as God loves.

HU *HYOO*   The most ancient, secret name for God. It can be sung as a love song to God aloud or silently to oneself to align with God's love.

initiation   Earned by a student of ECKANKAR through spiritual unfoldment and service to God. The initiation is a private ceremony in which the individual is linked to the Sound and Light of God.

Karma, Law of   The Law of Cause and Effect, action and reaction, justice, retribution, and reward, which applies to the lower or psychic worlds: the Physical, Astral, Causal, Mental, and Etheric PLANES.

Klemp, Harold   The present MAHANTA, the LIVING ECK MASTER. Sri Harold Klemp became the MAHANTA, the Living ECK Master in 1981. His spiritual name is WAH Z.

Living ECK Master   The spiritual leader of ECKANKAR. He leads SOUL back to God. He teaches in the physical world as the Outer Master, in the dream state as the Dream Master, and in the spiritual worlds as the Inner Master. SRI HAROLD KLEMP became the MAHANTA, the Living ECK Master in 1981.

MAHANTA   An expression of the Spirit of God that is always with you. Sometimes seen as a Blue Light or Blue Star or in the form of the MAHANTA, the LIVING ECK MASTER. The highest state of God Consciousness on earth, only embodied in the Living ECK Master. He is the Living Word.

261

planes Levels of existence, such as the Physical, Astral, Causal, Mental, Etheric, and Soul Planes.

Prajapati *prah-jah-PAH-tee* The ECK MASTER who cares for the animals.

Satsang A class in which students of ECK discuss a monthly lesson from ECKANKAR.

Self-Realization SOUL recognition. The entering of Soul into the Soul PLANE and there beholding Itself as pure Spirit. A state of Seeing, Knowing, and Being.

Shariyat-Ki-Sugmad Way of the Eternal; the sacred scriptures of ECKANKAR. The scriptures are comprised of twelve volumes in the spiritual worlds. The first two were transcribed from the inner PLANES by PAUL TWITCHELL, modern-day founder of Eckankar.

Soul The True Self, an individual, eternal spark of God. The inner, most sacred part of each person. Soul can see, know, and perceive all things. It is the creative center of Its own world.

Soul Travel The expansion of consciousness. The ability of SOUL to transcend the physical body and travel into the spiritual worlds of God. Soul Travel is taught only by the LIVING ECK MASTER. It helps people unfold spiritually and can provide proof of the existence of God and life after death.

Sound and Light of ECK The Holy Spirit. The two aspects through which God appears in the lower worlds. People can experience them by looking and listening within themselves and through SOUL TRAVEL.

Spiritual Exercises of ECK Daily practices for direct, personal experience with the God Current. Creative techniques using contemplation and the singing of sacred words to bring the higher awareness of SOUL into daily life.

Sri A title of spiritual respect, similar to reverend or pastor, used for those who have attained the Kingdom of God. In ECKANKAR, it is reserved for the MAHANTA, the LIVING ECK MASTER.

SUGMAD *SOOG-mahd* A sacred name for God. It is the source of all life, neither male nor female, the Ocean of Love and Mercy.

Temples of Golden Wisdom Golden Wisdom Temples found on the various PLANES—from the Physical to the Anami Lok; CHELAS of ECKANKAR are taken to these temples in the SOUL body to be educated in the divine knowledge; sections of the SHARIYAT-KI-SUGMAD, the sacred teachings of ECK, are kept at these temples.

Twitchell, Paul An American ECK MASTER who brought the modern teachings of ECKANKAR to the world through his writings and lectures. His spiritual name is Peddar Zaskq.

Wah Z *WAH zee* The spiritual name of Sri Harold Klemp. It means the secret doctrine. It is his name in the spiritual worlds.

For more explanations of Eckankar terms, see *A Cosmic Sea of Words: The ECKANKAR Lexicon*, by Harold Klemp.

263